MEET ME IN ST. LOUIS

Below are comments about Meet Me in St. Louis *that appeared on the dust jacket of the original hardcover edition in 1941:*

MEET ME IN SAINT LOUIS

BY SALLY BENSON

MEET ME IN SAINT LOUIS is the warm and nostalgic story of a typical American family in the year preceding the Saint Louis Exposition of 1904, told with all the skill and delightful humor that made Miss Benson's *Junior Miss* a Book-of-the-Month Club choice, a sensational hit on the stage, and a national radio feature for Shirley Temple.

The Smith family includes four daughters, ranging from seventeen-year-old Rose, "The Queen," to six-year-old Tootie, who is without question Miss Benson herself. Grandpa and the cook are also important parts of the household. The simple pleasures and problems of a day when most American families scarcely knew that a Germany or Japan existed will bring a reminiscent gleam to the eye of every reader over forty, and give the condescending younger generation an idea of some of the delightful things in life that it is missing altogether.

Meet Me in Saint Louis was one of the most successful features ever run in the pages of the *New Yorker Magazine*. Miss Benson is working now on the motion-picture version, which will be released for the Christmas holidays.

SALLY BENSON

MEET ME
IN
ST. LOUIS

St. Louis County Library thanks Barbara Benson Golseth and her children, Alexis Doster III, Sara T. Campbell, Robert W. Campbell, and Susan Campbell Ramsey, for making possible the reprint of *Meet Me in St. Louis*.

Meet Me in St. Louis
Copyright ©2004 Barbara Benson Golseth

All Rights Reserved
Published by Virginia Publishing Co.
For St. Louis County Library.

ISBN: 1-891442-26-0
Library of Congress Control Number: 2004104993

Originally published in hardcover, 1941, by the Random House Company, New York.

Cover design by Kimberly Fischer, St. Louis County Library.
Front cover photo: Stereoview, The Whiting View Company, Twentieth Century Series, No. 229 — Festival Hall, World's Fair St. Louis, Mo., 1904. Courtesy Diane Rademacher
Back cover photo of Sally Benson courtesy of Barbara Benson Golseth.

No part of this book may be reproduced in any form whatsoever without the expressed written consent of the copyright holder, except for a reviewer, who may quote brief passages in review.

Virginia Publishing Co.
P.O. Box 4538
St. Louis, MO 63108
(314) 367-6612
www.STL-BOOKS.com

Other books on the 1904 St. Louis World's Fair by Virginia Publishing Co.
Legacies of the World's Fair (1998)
Still Shining: Discovering Lost Treasures of the 1904 St. Louis World's Fair (2003)
Meeting Louis at the Fair: The Projects & Photographs of Louis Clemens Spiering, World's Fair Architect (2004)

THIS BOOK IS FOR
MY FAMILY

CONTENTS

	JUNE 1903	3
	JULY 1903	33
	AUGUST 1903	55
	SEPTEMBER 1903	79
	OCTOBER 1903	101
	NOVEMBER 1903	125
	DECEMBER 1903	151
	JANUARY 1904	175
	FEBRUARY 1904	197
	MARCH 1904	223
	APRIL 1904	243
	MAY 1904	269

June 1903

JUNE 1903

Tootie Smith was awake, but she lay in bed without opening her eyes. She could tell it was a sunny day by the light which shone through her eyelids. It was a bright-orange shade, and she knew that the room was flooded with sunlight. On rainy days the light that came through her eyelids was a dark purplish brown. She stretched her thin little legs and felt the scab, a really good one, on one knee with her hand.

There were two doors to her room, one leading to a large, square, central hall and the other leading to a back bedroom, where her mother and father slept. The doors were open, and Tootie could feel the hot summer breeze as it blew across her bare legs and could hear the window shades moving back and forth with a sucking sound. In her parents' room, someone was walking about quietly, and she heard the screen being raised in one of the back windows. "It's Lon," she thought. "And he's going to tell me that thing about the pony again."

She waited for him to speak. "Well!" he said. "I'll be doggoned!"

Tootie set her lips and kept her eyes tightly shut.

"I'll be doggoned!" Lon repeated. "Well, that's a good one on me! Who'd ever think it? Here I was yesterday playing a joke on poor little Tootie, telling her there was a pony in the back yard, and darned if it doesn't come true!"

His voice was filled with excitement, and Tootie stirred uneasily in her bed.

"Tootie," he called softly.

She didn't answer, and he came into her room, calling her again.

She opened her eyes and looked at him. His bright-blue eyes were shining and his light-brown hair was damp where he had wet it to keep down the cowlick that grew on the crown of his head. He wore white duck trousers, spotted with grass stains, and a white shirt open at the neck. "Tootie," he said. "What do you think?"

"There isn't," she said.

"Isn't what?"

"Isn't a pony in the back yard."

He walked over to the window, jingling the coins in his pocket and frowning. "I was afraid of that." He pretended to be talking to himself. "Afraid she wouldn't believe me. I should have known. Shouldn't have said anything." He sighed. "Of course," he went on, "I deserve it after the lie I told her yesterday. Anyone who would tell a lie to a little six-year-old girl is a cad."

"I don't believe it," Tootie said.

He turned to face her. "And why should you?" he asked. "It's nothing short of a miracle. Yesterday, I admit, there was *not* a pony in the back yard. I played you a dirty trick. I'm ashamed of myself—a man of eighteen deceiving a little child. Why, I wouldn't blame you, Tootie, if you never spoke to me again. I wouldn't blame you if you never even wrote me next winter, when I'll be thousands of miles away from St. Louis in Princeton, New Jersey, alone and without friends in the bitter cold."

Tootie smiled. "I didn't really mind about yesterday," she said. "And I got some candy with the dime. Is it really so cold in Princeton?"

"Colder than Greenland, they tell me," he said. "And snow as high as this house."

"Gosh!" she cried. "How will you get to school?"

"On sleds," he said. "That is, the freshmen have to use sleds, but the seniors use dog teams." He moved toward the door. "I think I'll tell Agnes about that pony. She's always wanted one."

"Is there a pony?" Tootie asked. "Is there, *really*?"

"You have my word for it," he said. "A white pony. Snowy white, with a little saddle that looked to me as though it were studded with gems. Imitations, I suppose. But they certainly shone like real."

"A white pony," Tootie repeated. "Yesterday you told me a black pony."

He bowed his head. "*That* was a lie."

She sat up and lifted the mosquito netting that hung like a canopy over her bed. It smelled strongly of oil of pennyroyal. She slid under it and stood on the dark-green carpet in her bare feet. Her nightgown was too short for her and came just below her knees. Her shins were a mass of bruises. Last night her mother had twisted her hair into a knot on the top of her head and pinned it with a large bone hairpin. But the hairpin had become loosened and her hair hung down curly and damp at the nape of her neck.

"Going to look at him?" Lon asked.

"No," she said. "I think you're fooling."

"Well, it's up to you," he said. He went out into the hall, and she could hear him running down the stairs. "Say, Mamma!" he called. "Have you a piece of good, stout rope?"

Tootie tiptoed to the hall door and closed it. Then she walked softly into the back bedroom in her bare feet. The screen in the window was still open, and for a moment she stood staring at it, torn with doubt and sick with apprehension. If there was a pony in the back yard and she didn't claim him first, Rose or Esther or Agnes might see him, and she would miss the opportunity of a lifetime. Lon had sworn there was. She walked slowly to the open window and leaned out.

The yard to the house at 5135 Kensington

Avenue stretched back about three hundred feet to the alley, down which the trolley cars ran. At the end of the yard, facing the house, were a brick-and-cement ashpit and a two-story clapboard woodshed and chicken house. Her eyes travelled over every foot of the yard. There were the wooden walk that led from the house to the woodshed, the canvas hammock under the big maple tree; there were the row of cherry trees, the pear tree, and the two peach trees; there were the lilac bush, the clump of peonies, the rosebushes, and the snowball bush; there was the lawn of grass and red and white clover; but there was no pony.

She let the screen down gently and went back to her room, which she shared with Agnes. She noticed that Agnes had made her bed. She thought that Agnes must have moved very quietly, and wondered if Lon had laughed with Agnes about the pony while she lay asleep. She slipped her nightgown over her head and pulled on a pair of white drawers with starched ruffles. The apron she had worn yesterday hung on a hook in the wardrobe. She put it on, fastening the two buttons at the back of the neck but leaving the bow at the back of her waist untied. A vision of the white pony still danced before her eyes. She could see the curve of his proud head and the way he stamped his small feet. She saw the jewels of his saddle sparkling in the sun. Her eyes clouded with tears as she stooped to pick up her sandals, and as she slid one foot into the right sandal, her toes touched a wad of paper. There was a quarter wrapped in the paper and a poem written on it. She put the quarter in her apron pocket and read the poem. It said:

> *Tootie is a bad girl,*
> *Tootie is a fraud,*
> *Tootie is the worst girl*
> *I ever sawed.*

Rose was sitting in the sliding swing on the front porch when Tootie went downstairs. She was reading a letter, and by the number of stamps on the envelope Tootie could tell it was a special-delivery letter. The air was sweet with the scent of the honeysuckle vine that grew over the porch. When Rose looked up from her letter her soft-brown eyes were kind. "He ought to be ashamed of himself," she said.

"Who?" Tootie asked.

"Lon."

"Oh!" Tootie laughed. "You mean about the pony. I knew he was only fooling. I didn't even look."

"Well, I'm glad," Rose said. "I told him you were too smart to fool twice in succession. Back up here and I'll tie your bow. And you'd better not let Mamma catch you with your hair uncombed."

Rose didn't tie a pretty bow. Esther tied the best bows. But Tootie stood patiently while Rose fumbled with it and then combed Tootie's hair with one of her own side combs. When she had finished, Tootie sat down beside her on the swing, moving one of the cushions, a tan leather one on which was burned the head of an Indian girl. It was Tootie's favorite pillow, because the Indian girl's headband was made of real red and green stones sewed to the leather.

Rose finished reading her letter and put her arm around Tootie. "Well, if he isn't the silliest man!" she said. "Really, sometimes I think he's lost his mind."

"What's he done now?" Tootie asked. She bounded up and down on the swing. "Tell me! Tell me!"

ST. LOUIS *June 1903*

Since John Shepard had entered the life of the Smith family when he'd come all the way from New Haven to spend the Christmas holidays with Harry Dodge over five months ago, he had been a fascinating topic of discussion. For one thing, he was a junior at Yale and lived in New York, and for another, his father was a judge. The first night he had called on Rose, all the family had discreetly disappeared, and Mr. Smith had even closed the folding doors between the parlor and the dining room, where he sat playing solitaire. Of course, Mr. Smith had asked his usual question when Rose told him that a boy named John Shepard was coming to call. "Never heard of him," he said, wetting the end of his cigar with his tongue. "What does his father do?"

He had merely grunted when Rose told him that John's father was a judge, but he had closed the folding doors, which was more than he had ever done before. Mrs. Smith had hoped that Rose wouldn't take the thing too seriously, but she called up Miss Thibault, the dressmaker, and together they had made a new dress for Rose. Esther thought that John was wonderful for no profounder reasons than that he wore trousers and went to Yale. Even **Agnes**, who didn't like anybody, merely said that he hadn't any chin. "He's better than that Harry Dodge, though," she added. "*He looks like a dish of melted strawberry ice cream.*"

Lon couldn't understand what John Shepard saw in Rose, and Grandpa Prophater pretended he couldn't remember John Shepard's name and called him Mr. Dodge and Mr. Riley. When the holidays were over and John went back to New Haven, letters began to come—two or three days apart at first. But now they came daily, special delivery, and Esther had discovered that the letters began "Dear Siddums," a nickname that John had made up from Rose's middle name, which was Sidney. He had introduced new words and Esther and Rose had added them to their vocabulary. Things were now "keen" and people were no longer "folks" but "folk." So Tootie knew that if Rose thought John Shepard had lost his mind, he must be going to do something very spectacular indeed. It must be something more than sending flowers and ten-pound boxes of Page & Shaw candy. "What's he done now?" she repeated.

"He's going to telephone," Rose said. "Telephone long-distance from New York."

Tootie gasped. "Does Mamma know?" she asked. "Can I tell her?"

"You *may* tell her," Rose answered. "He's phoning at half past eight. Goodness knows what I'm going to do. I have an engagement with Joe Riley for eight."

"Break it, Rose! Break it!" Tootie begged.

Rose put her hand up to her hair and smoothed her pompadour. "I'll see," she said. "You'd better get your breakfast."

"It's too hot to eat," Tootie said. "I'll eat some plums." She bounced up and ran into the house.

Rose sat still in the swing, holding John Shepard's letter in her hand. She thought of the way his hair curled, crisp and tight on his head, of his eyes, which were cool and gray and almost cold at times; she remembered the way his hands looked and how his pipe smelled. But most of all she wondered what he was going to say to her when he telephoned tonight. He would never, she thought, spend all that money just to say hello, although he had written he wanted to hear her voice. Yet it seemed to her that a telephone call from New York was almost as good as a proposal.

The sun shining through the honeysuckle vine made a dark design on her white linen skirt. She could hear the sound of the lawnmower in the side yard, and knew her mother had found out that Lon had fooled Tootie again and had set him to work. She got up and went into the front hall. It was dark and cool and smelled of the wax that Katie used to polish the parquet floor, which was dotted with Oriental scatter rugs. Against the left wall was an upright piano with an elaborately carved front faced with a square of green baize. The baize was punctured with holes where the children had pushed their fingers through it. There was a piano stool covered with green velvet and green-and-rose brocaded satin portières hung in the wide doorway that led to the parlor. Beside the doorway was a heavy, round mahogany table on which was set a Tiffany glass bowl and a silver card tray filled with calling cards. In the back of the hall, on another table, was a Sheffield water-cooler lined with porcelain; a silver goblet was under the faucet.

ST. LOUIS *June 1903*

Rose walked to the water-cooler, turned on the faucet, and drank from the goblet before she started up the stairs. The stair carpet had been taken off for the summer, and her heels clicked on the shiny wood. She held lightly to the banister until she reached the landing. The landing was wide enough for a corner table, and on the table was a bowl of old-fashioned white roses that looked mottled in the light that shone through the stained-glass window. She picked a rose from the bowl and tucked it in her hair. It was unfortunate that at this moment Grandpa Prophater should start down the stairs. His hair was white and thick and his eyebrows were black and startling. Underneath them his black eyes were bright with malice. "The Queen!" he said.

He had a weird and amazing variety of hats, and today he wore a scarlet Turkish fez decorated with a black tassel. He bowed as Rose passed him. "The Queen," he repeated.

She walked up the rest of the stairs and turned to the right to enter the large front room that belonged to her and Esther. It was an elegant room, with pale-blue wallpaper which was striped with silver, and glossy bird's-eye-maple furniture, a chaise longue, and white ruffled curtains tied with pale-blue bows. Esther was dressing. She was small and dark, and her dimples showed when she smiled. "Ess," Rose said, "get away from that window. People can see you."

"They won't know it's me," Esther said. "They'll think it's you. Did Tootie bite?"

"I can't see," Rose said, "how you can all spend your time thinking up ways to fool Tootie. I should think it would be beneath you."

Esther turned to stare at her. "Why, *you* do it. You do it yourself. You thought of the one about the buried treasure."

"That was last summer," Rose said.

"It was last September," Esther reminded her. "And you thought of a lot of things April Fools' Day. You even pinned the sign on her back."

"Well, I think it's childish now," Rose said. "And I must say that if I were married and had children, I wouldn't want them teased to death."

Esther slipped a white middy blouse over her head. "Imagine you married and having a lot of children!" she said.

ST. LOUIS *June 1903*

"It's not impossible," Rose said. "Grandma Prophater was married when she was sixteen, and I'm seventeen. I think it's nice to marry young and be young with your children." She walked over to her bureau and began arranging her silver toilet set. Her mother had given it to her on her sixteenth birthday, but Tootie had scratched "R.S.S." on each piece with a pin and it had lost some of its original elegance.

"John's phoning me tonight," Rose said.

Esther's mouth opened slightly and she gasped. "Phoning you," she said. "*Now* I see! Now I see why you're talking about getting married and being so funny about Tootie. And if you ask me, I think it's just a pose."

"When you are my age, you'll feel differently. Besides, I don't see why you assume that John is going to propose to me tonight."

"What else would he be phoning for?" Esther asked. "Why else would he be spending all that money? Bob didn't phone Mary Finley until after they were engaged. Not long-distance. Are you engaged?"

"I'm not exactly engaged and I'm not exactly *not* engaged. Anyway, it seems to me that one little phone call is causing an awful lot of

17

excitement," Rose said. "Of course, I'll have to break an engagement with Joe Riley to be here to get the call."

"Break an engagement with Joe after he gave you a collie!" Esther cried. "A perfectly beautiful collie!"

"He was a beautiful collie," Rose agreed. Tears came to her eyes, but she brushed them away. "He died, though," she said.

"John's perfectly grand," Esther said. She pinned a red bow on the back of her hair. "At least, he seems grand. Not that we really know him, though."

"I know him," Rose said. "And that's all that's necessary." She walked out of the room and across the hall to her mother's room.

Mrs. Smith was making the large double bed. It was a black-walnut bed with a high headboard and it matched the bureau and the washstand. The floor was covered with a darkbrown figured carpet that had once been the parlor carpet. The room had a fireplace with an asbestos gas grate, a mahogany wardrobe, a small golden-oak rocker with low arms, a Morris chair with black leather cushions, and two straight chairs that had belonged to the dining-room set and were sometimes carried downstairs to be used when company came for dinner.

Mrs. Smith was small and compact. She wore her hair gathered into a knot on top of her head. Before she had married Mr. Smith, she had worn bangs, which she curled with an iron. They had given her hair a faint scorched smell. It was a smell that Mr. Smith missed, just as he missed the way they used to go out together. When Lon was born, Mrs. Smith didn't seem to care to go out any more, to the summer gardens or to play whist at the Friday Night Whist Club. She was, she said, afraid something would happen to the baby. And, as there was always a baby, she almost always decided to stay home. Night after night Mr. Smith sat at the dining-room table playing double-deck solitaire while his wife put the children to bed. Twice a week Frank Casey came to play cribbage with Mr. Smith. The two men sat silently, and Mrs. Smith frowned a little at the pitcher of beer that stood on the table beside the cribbage board and listened to the monotonous counting, "Fifteen-two, fifteen-four, and four is eight." On the top of her bureau was a bottle of Guerlain's Jicky, and in the top drawer was a box of rice powder and a Roger & Gallet cardboard lipstick. The lipstick was a pale pink, and Mrs. Smith insisted that she used it to keep her lips from chapping. Still, there was no doubt that the lipstick gave her lips a deeper shade.

As Rose entered the room, Mrs. Smith looked up at her. "Have you and Esther made your bed?" she asked.

"Yes, Mamma," Rose answered.

"Tootie told me about the phone call you're expecting tonight," Mrs. Smith said. She thumped a pillow energetically. "If I were you, I wouldn't commit myself one way or the other."

Rose's face turned scarlet. "Oh, I don't think—" she began.

"I don't believe in long engagements," her mother said. "Your father and I were only engaged for six months. He gave me my ring in May and we were married in October. Besides, you know very little about John Shepard. We've never even met his folks. He *says* his father is a judge, and I don't doubt but it's so. Nevertheless—"

ST. LOUIS *June 1903*

"I thought you liked him," Rose said.

"I like him well enough, but I think you're too young to commit yourself. Besides, I don't think your father will allow it."

Rose thought of her father, silent, growing a little round-shouldered, and couldn't remember when he hadn't allowed anything. She smiled to herself. "Well, I'm going over to Abby's," she said. "And I'll call Joe Riley from there."

"I feel sorry for poor Joe," her mother said.

There was decidedly an atmosphere in the house the rest of the day. At noon, Rose telephoned to say that she was staying for lunch with Abby Means, and it was generally understood that she was avoiding the issue. Lon finished cutting the lawn and spent the rest of the long, hot afternoon batting a tennis ball against the side of the brick house. Esther shut herself into her room to write letters. Agnes and Corinne Lacey, her best friend, sat under the big maple tree and played with their paperdoll houses. Tootie was missing. She had gone off with the iceman again, Mrs. Smith thought. Tootie and Helen Ferris, with whom she played, went away with the iceman every chance they had. They rode on the small step on the back of the wagon, ate the ice chips until they were ready to burst, and helped the iceman brush the sawdust from the hundred-pound cakes.

Grandpa Prophater, when he heard the news about the telephone call, put on his hat and went down to the levee. He always went there when he was disturbed about something. At one time he had owned three boats that ran from St. Louis to New Orleans, and he found peace sitting around and talking to the men down at the levee.

Mrs. Smith broke her rule about never telephoning Mr. Smith at the office. "Lonnie," she said, "that John Shepard is going to phone Rose long-distance from New York tonight."

Mr. Smith took it calmly. "Some people have more money than sense," he said.

Even Katie didn't go up to her room on the top floor for her afternoon nap; instead she took out her feelings by baking three cherry pies and two dozen cinnamon buns.

Agnes and Tootie were the only ones who talked very much at the dinner table. Tootie still sat in her old high chair, from which the tray had been removed. "The iceman saw a man get shot," she said. "He was a drunken man and the blood spurted out at least three feet."

"Not at the table, Tootie," her mother said. "And eat your mashed potatoes."

"Can I eat them my way?" Tootie asked. "I don't think I can choke them down unless I eat them my way."

Tootie's way was to squeeze her mashed potatoes in her fist until they came out like fat white worms between her fingers.

"You cannot," her mother said. She didn't mention the fact that Tootie had not touched her peas, as it was generally understood that Tootie didn't like any vegetables but beets and that she only liked beets because they were red.

Agnes sat primly at her mother's left. She wore a black-and-white plaid gingham dress and a white guimpe. Her delicate fingers held her fork daintily. "I finished the art gallery in my paper-doll house today," she said. "My family have mostly Rembrandts. They have 'The Laughing Cavalier,' too."

"'Smiling Cavalier,'" Rose said.

"'Laughing,'" Agnes persisted. "They have the 'Mona Lisa' and two Corots."

"Tomorrow I'm going to work on my

paper-doll house," Tootie said. "I'm going to cut out some more autos for the garage." Tootie's paper-doll family were named Rockefeller, because Lon had told her they were the richest family in the world.

"By the way," Lon said, "I read in the paper today that Mrs. Rockerfeller has hydrophobia."

"I'll put her to bed," Tootie said. "I'll cut out a chest for her room and paste medicine bottles in it. I'll cut out a man for a doctor. The man I had for a doctor got torn when the children had chicken pox. Is hydrophobia bad? I wouldn't want Mrs. Rockerfeller to die."

"A poodle bit her," Lon said. "She may die."

Tootie's mouth quivered.

"Don't pay any attention to him," Rose said. "He's making it up."

The Smiths ate later in the summer and it was after eight when they got up from the table. Usually Mr. and Mrs. Smith and Grandpa Prophater sat on the long green bench that stood on the lawn near the terrace, where they could see and speak to the people who passed by. But tonight, although it was hot, they sat in the parlor, talking softly. Tootie and Agnes went up to the upstairs hall and sat on the floor, so that they would be sure to be there when the telephone rang, and Esther said something about straightening her bureau drawers.

"I don't know what's got into everybody tonight," Rose said. She went out of the house and banged the door, and they could hear the sliding swing as it creaked back and forth. Pretty soon Lon joined her. "Katie's sitting on the back stairs," he told her, and laughed.

"How perfectly absurd!" Rose said.

The house seemed very still. Outside, people strolled by and children laughed and screamed. The sky had clouded over and the grass on the lawn seemed to turn a bright-green shade, the way it did before a storm.

Suddenly the ringing of the telephone broke the stillness. There was a rush for the stairs, and Tootie began to shiver with excitement. Katie crept up the back stairs to the top step. Rose got up slowly from the swing and walked upstairs. The family fell back and made an aisle for her as she went to the telephone.

"Hello," she said.

There was a long pause and she could hear

the operator saying "All right, Chicago," and the Chicago operator saying "All right, New York."

The New York operator asked, "Is this St. Louis, Forrest 840? New York is calling Miss Rose Smith. Miss Rose Smith."

"This is Miss Rose Smith speaking," Rose said.

There was another pause, and then she heard John's voice. "Hello, Rose? Siddums?" he asked.

Rose wondered if the operator could hear that he called her Siddums. "Hello, John," she said.

"How are you? How are you, Siddums?"

Rose felt the eight pairs of eyes at her back. "It's awfully hot," she said.

"It's hot here, too. Not as hot as it is there, though, I guess."

"It's pretty hot," she said. "Almost as hot as July." John's voice sounded strange, as though he were talking down into a well.

"I can't hear you very well," Rose said.

"That's funny," he said. "I can hear you fine."

"What did you want?" Rose asked.

"Well," he said, "there are a lot of things

I want to say. Is anybody listening?" There was a note of caution in his voice. "I made the call for tonight because all my people are out. You know how they are."

"No," Rose said, "I don't."

"Well, they're funny," he said. "I suppose there'll be 'h' to pay when they find out I've called you."

"How strange!" Rose said. "My family are all home. They didn't think anything of it."

"It's a little different from their angle," he said.

"Well," Rose said, "I'd better not waste any more of your time and money."

"Hey, wait a minute!" he shouted.

"I can't talk any longer," she said. "I have an engagement. I think I hear Joe's voice now." She stood holding the receiver to her ear, but John did not speak. "Goodbye," she said. "Thanks a lot for calling."

"I'll write you tonight, Siddums," he said.

"Do that little thing," she said. "So long."

She put the receiver back on its hook and turned to face her family. Her father looked at her slyly. "More money than sense," he said.

Rose went into her room and heard the

others file slowly down the stairs. She heard the screen door open and close, and heard her mother and father and Grandpa Prophater as they settled themselves on the bench on the lawn. Katie began to bang the pans in the kitchen and run the water in the sink. Lon slipped a dime into Agnes' hand. "Get yourself a soda," he said. Rose could hear Tootie screaming as she slid down the terrace to the sidewalk, and heard Esther picking at the piano, playing "Never Mind What They Call You, Darling."

She sat down in front of her dressing table and stared at her face in the mirror, trying to remember what she and John had talked about at Christmas time, but she couldn't remember a word he had said, only the way he had looked. Usually at this time she went to her desk to write him a letter. He expected a letter every day. But tonight she didn't feel like writing, somehow. She sat there until it grew dark outside, and then she got up and turned on the light. Moths and June bugs beat against the screen, and this familiar sound and the sight of her room with its lovely bird's-eye-maple furniture gave her the impression that

ST. LOUIS *June 1903*

she was home again after a long journey. It was too late to phone Joe Riley and, besides, she had told him that she wasn't well. She walked to the door and called downstairs to Esther. Esther stopped picking at the piano and ran quickly up the stairs.

"Listen, Ess," she said. "I have a wonderful idea. Where's Margaretha?"

Margaretha was Tootie's favorite doll.

"I think I saw her on the back porch before supper, in her carriage," Esther said. "Why?"

"Well, go get her and we'll hide her in our closet. We'll kidnap her and leave a ransom note for Tootie."

Esther laughed and her dimples flashed. "Oh, grand!" she said. "Grand!" She ran out of the room and down the back stairs.

"And tell Lon!" Rose called after her. She went over to the desk and tore a page from a loose-leaf notebook. Then, taking a small paintbrush from the desk drawer, she dipped it in the ink and began to print on the lined paper. "TOOTIE SMITH," she wrote. "MARGARETHA IS IN THE HANDS OF HER TORTURERS. UNLESS YOU PAY TEN DOLLARS IN CRISP NEW

June 1903

ONE-DOLLAR BILLS BY SUNDOWN TONIGHT, SHE WILL DIE! ! !" She signed it "MAFIA," and drew a large, black hand at the bottom of the page.

Esther came into the room with Margaretha in her arms. "I stuffed some wood under the blanket in case Tootie looked," she said.

"Yes," Rose said. "I think it's the best idea yet. We won't leave the note until tomorrow morning, or there'll be hell to pay."

"Rose!" Esther said. "You swore."

"So I did," Rose answered, and laughed. New York seemed very far away.

July 1903

JULY 1903

It was after eleven o'clock in the evening, and Mr. Smith sat at the dining-room table playing solitaire. Even though he had opened the door that led to the back porch, the room was close, and from time to time he glanced irritably at the folding doors, which he had shut earlier in the evening because the noise from the living room was more than he could bear. The portières that hung across the folding doors had been taken down for the summer; the lace curtains had been washed, dried on stretchers in the back yard, and packed away; even the silver coffee service and the cut-glass punch bowl, which usually sat on the sideboard, were gone, and the whole dining room had a deserted look. His cards stuck to the shiny surface of the golden-oak table.

He had closed the folding doors the instant Roy Dunham and Warren Bogart came to call on the girls. They had brought the latest hits of the Rogers Brothers' show with them, and for a while his feelings had been harrowed as his daughter Rose played the songs over on the piano, at first faltering a little and then dashing them off brilliantly. They all sang, except Lon, who accompanied them on his mandolin. Now they had stopped playing, and it seemed to Mr. Smith that Rose and Esther were doing most of the talking. He gathered up his cards, shuffled them, and laid them out once more on the table. At the end of this game, he thought, I will go out and wind the clock.

"What do you think?" he heard Rose say. "I met Mr. Peters in the drugstore before dinner. Wasn't Blanche a heartless wretch to jilt him?"

"Well, I think it's a perfect shame," Esther said. "Just think, it was just a year ago that their case was at its height."

"It's quite touching to see him wearing the ring Blanche used to sport," Rose said. "I guess he's still single hearted and fancy-free."

Mr. Smith moved uneasily in his chair. He loved his pretty daughters, and it seemed to him that when there were no outsiders they talked intelligently at times. It was only when the boys dropped in that they changed; their voices were too sweet, their laughter was shrill and affected. He now heard Tootie's voice, which added to his nervousness. Tootie was only six. She must have come downstairs in her nightgown, he thought.

"Rose and Esther say there's a divine boy that's moved in across the street," Tootie said. "Esther and Rose are crazy about him."

Mr. Smith heard the boys' laughter and the screaming protests of the girls. He got up and walked toward the folding doors, peering through the crack into the living room. Tootie was sitting on her brother Lon's lap. She had a nightgown on and her feet were bare. Her hair was curly and damp from the heat and her eyes shone with the excitement of being downstairs so late. Lon whispered something in her ear. "Rose says he wears such cute pants," she announced, "and has the real Smith Academy walk."

"That's enough, Tootie," Rose said firmly. "You go back to bed or I'll call Mamma."

"Mamma doesn't care," Tootie said. "She's packing. She *told* me to come down. She says to tell you that there's a whole pile of clothes on your bed waiting to be packed. She says to tell you remember that you have to get up at six."

Lon reached for one of the pralines the girls had made that afternoon and Tootie's mouth opened like a bird's. He broke a piece off and flipped it into her mouth. Then she tilted her head so that Lon could whisper in her ear again.

"Oh, yes," she said. "Esther says he's an Apolla and she's written volumes of poetry in his honor."

Mr. Smith walked away from the doors and went into the kitchen. Katie was packing potato salad into glass jars for the box lunch that Mrs. Smith, Lon, and the girls were to take with them on the train tomorrow. On the table beside the jars was a cardboard box full of fried chicken wrapped in wax paper. "Katie," Mr. Smith said, "Tootie's still up."

"I believe it," Katie said calmly. "And I bet she has a bold face on her." She screwed the top tightly on a glass jar and wiped the sides with a damp cloth.

ST. LOUIS *July 1903*

"That potato salad looks all right," Mr. Smith said. "I wish I were going with them."

"I saved some out for your lunch tomorrow," Katie said.

He walked to the back hall and was about to call up the stairs when his twelve-year-old daughter Agnes started down them. She was hauling a doll's carriage after her, and as she reached the landing she began to scream. "Katie! Where's my cat? Where is she?"

Katie glanced over to the rocking chair to where Lady Babbie, a fat, gray alley cat, was sleeping. "I don't know where she is," she answered. "A while back she got in my way, and I kicked her down the cellar steps, and I could hear her spine hit on every step."

Agnes's screams grew louder, and Mr. Smith stood aside as she banged the carriage against the wall and ran into the kitchen. "If you've killed her," she cried, standing in front of Katie, "I'll kill you! I'll stab you to death in your sleep, and then I'll tie your body to two wild horses until you're pulled apart."

"Won't that be terrible, now?" Katie said. She nodded toward the rocking chair. "There's your cat."

Agnes ran over to the chair and picked up Lady Babbie. She buried her face in the cat's soft fur, wiping the tears from her cheeks. She carried the cat to the doll's carriage and laid her gently down, covering her with a doll's sheet and fastening the leather strap tightly, so that Lady Babbie would not be able to get out. "I'm going to wheel her out onto the back porch," she said. "It's too hot for her in the house tonight."

She opened the screen door and slid carefully out, wheeling the carriage to the far end of the porch, where it was cooler. She bent down and kissed Lady Babbie on the mouth. When she came back into the kitchen, she took a small piece of paper from her pocket. "I wrote out a few instructions, Katie," she said. "About what to do for Lady Babbie while I'm gone. I thought because tomorrow will be the first day, she should have some extra things. Because she's going to miss me awfully." She fished in her pocket once more and brought out a dime. "This is for a can of sardines. It's enough to buy a can of sardines, isn't it?"

"That's a funny thing," Katie said. "I was noticing just tonight that there's a can of sardines in the cupboard. And I was thinking that they'd spoil sure before you all come back. You keep your dime." She wiped her hand on her apron and hit Agnes softly on her shoulder. Then she took the piece of paper and hung it on a screw over the sink. "That's so it'll be where I can see it," she said.

"Thank you a million times," Agnes said. "I think she'll be all right for tonight, don't you?"

Katie heard the sound of Lady Babbie's feet as they hit the floor of the porch. "Oh, sure," she said. "She'll be fine, all covered up out there. She'll never open an eye till morning."

"Anna," Mr. Smith called softly up the back stairs. His wife did not answer, and he called again. The back hall was very hot and smelled of the rubbers and overshoes that were piled at the bottom of the hatrack. He walked back through the kitchen into the dining room. The living room was empty now, and he could hear voices in the front hall, and then the sound of the screen door as it banged shut. He opened the folding doors. The furniture in the living room had been covered neatly with old sheets that were mussed and wrinkled where they had been sat on. Esther and Rose had started up the stairs, their arms around each other's waists, and Lon was putting his mandolin back into its case. The case was covered with Smith Academy stickers of red and white and Princeton stickers of orange and black, although Lon would not enter Princeton until the fall. Mr. Smith sat down in a chair by the wide living-room window and took a cigar from his pocket. He slid the band off carefully, without thinking, because Agnes was saving them this year. Last year, Esther had saved them. There was a slight breeze near the window, and he put his head back and closed his eyes.

Upstairs, Mrs. Smith crossed the hall into the girls' room. "I don't know what you could have been dreaming of," she said sharply. "Look at that bed! And after dancing all last night. I'm speaking to *you*, Rose. I must say I think it was extremely thoughtless of Mr. Dunham and Mr. Bogart to stay so late. Couldn't you have told them the hack will be here at half past seven?"

ST. LOUIS *July 1903*

She gave a hurried glance around the room. The bed was piled high with clothes that were to go in the suitcases. That morning the expressman had taken the trunks to the depot, where they had been checked and sent on ahead. The trunks sometimes didn't arrive until two or three days after the family had arrived in Manitowoc, Wisconsin, where Grandma and Grandpa Smith lived, and Mrs. Smith had discovered that it was practical to take as many clean dresses, clean petticoats, and underclothes as could be crammed into the suitcases. She vaguely distrusted the way the railroad handled trunks.

"We'll do them, Mamma," Rose said. "We'll do them right away."

"Well," Mrs. Smith said, "Tootie and Agnes are packed, anyway. Tootie's taking all her dolls, even the little ones. She says she's going to have a cemetery again near the asparagus bed, so I think she's just taking them along to bury them. Your father wired Grandma Smith."

"Wired her about the dolls?" Esther asked.

"Certainly not," Mrs. Smith said. "He simply wired the exact time."

"It's awfully embarrassing with Tootie and Agnes," Esther said. "The stuff they take, all those dolls and books, and the way they drink water."

"Well, Miss," her mother said, "don't forget that I went through the same thing with you."

She left the room and Rose closed the door after her and threw herself onto the bed among all the clothes. "I don't think I can stand leaving. It'll be too deadly leaving this time. Just when we've almost got to meet Frank Hodgen."

"I know," Esther said. "And I heard loads more about him today from Mrs. Wagner."

"What did you hear, *enfant*?" Rose asked. She had taken to calling Esther *enfant* ever since she had got ninety-five on her final French examination.

"Well," Esther said, "he's the president of his class at Smith Academy."

"Oh, I knew *that*. Lon told me."

"Well, he's captain of the track team, and the *best* of all is that he can do the hundred-and-twenty-yard hurdle in sixteen and three-fifths seconds."

"Don't you just love it?" Rose said. "Now I'll tell *you* something. Helen Morse used to eat at the same boarding house with him and his mother, and I have found out, one, that he is quiet but is being constantly disgraced by his mother, who used to tell all his affairs in front of the whole boarding-house. And, two, that two weeks ago he had but one decent suit to his name, and his mother said, 'I'm afraid Frank will have to go to bed while his suit is at the cleaner's.'"

"How detestable!" Esther said. "I should think he'd drop through the floor."

"And, *three*," Rose went on, "that Mrs. H. said, 'Frankie was born at Rye Beach, New Hampshire. He is a real little Yankee lad.' And, *four*, that one time, when he wanted to have his new suit with a military coat and wide pants, his mother raised strenuous objections and spluttered half an hour about it, until Frank said, 'Now, Fatty, don't get excited,' and then ordered the suit the way he wanted it."

"He would, too," Esther said. "It's just what he would do."

"But the worst is yet to come," Rose said.

"Mrs. Wagner *told* Mrs. Hodgen that we were smitten with Frank, and now Mrs. H. goes around saying that she hears Frankie has made a hit with the young ladies across the street, quite good-looking girls, too. She said it in front of Frank when they were out one night, and everyone said, 'Dear me,' and Frank blushed and glued his eyes to his plate."

"I'm glad we're going," Esther said. "I could never face him again after that."

"Oh, I don't know," Rose said. "I heard that for all his bashfulness, he is awfully spoony. I heard it from a reliable authority. Margaret Dodge verified this, because she knows a girl who knows him, and he said to her one night that he thought the Black River was a daisy place, and that he could hardly keep from proposing to the girl he was with every time he rowed down the river in the moonlight."

"Well, even if I can't face him again, ever, I'm glad Lon ran up to him at the Interscholastic Field Day and shook hands with him after he had won his hurdle and was third in his high jump."

"I'm glad, too," Rose said. She got up

from the bed and loosened the pins in her hair. "Well, I suppose we must think of *le matin.*"

Together they dragged the suitcases down from the closet shelf and opened them on the floor. "I wonder who'll be at Manitowoc this year. I wish we could go to South Haven," Esther said. "Everybody we know goes there."

Rose lifted a pile of underwear from the bed and arranged the pieces at the bottom of a suitcase. "I love our new sacques," she said. "And I think it's perfectly thrilling about Lon's tuxedo. But I could cry when I think of where I'll ever get a chance to wear my heavenly dress." The dress was Rose's pride. It was made of a new grass-cloth material embroidered with forget-me-nots. The yoke was of thin, tucked Holland linen and ecru lace, and had two straps of Holland linen crossing at the bottom. She had covered these straps and all other plain places with blue French knots. Miss Thibault, the dressmaker, had designed the dress herself, with a few suggestions from Mrs. Smith, but the French knots were Rose's own particular idea, and she had worked on them for days.

"I suppose Chet Murphy will be at the

station when we get there," Esther said. "And Jewett Ottmar."

"Poor Jewett Ottmar," Rose said. "It must be dreadful to have only one eye."

"Yes," Esther said gravely. "But the other is a perfectly beautiful shade of brown."

"We'd better get a move on," Rose said. "I think I hear Mamma again."

Mrs. Smith came downstairs from the third floor, where she had been helping Lon finish with his packing. It was generally understood that the two older girls could do their own packing but that Lon, Agnes, and Tootie couldn't—Lon because he was a young man, and Tootie and Agnes because they weren't to be trusted. She passed the girls' room, noticed that they were quiet and therefore must be doing as they had been told, and went on to the children's room. The room was dark. Mrs. Smith listened for a moment, and then closed the door quietly.

"I bet you don't remember Sue and Jenny," Agnes said, continuing the conversation, which had been interrupted when they heard their mother's footsteps.

"I do, too," Tootie said. "They're pillows. The red-and-white one is Sue, and she's mine. And the blue-and-white one is yours."

"Do you remember riding on the bus?" Agnes asked.

Tootie frowned in the dark. "Where?"

"In Chicago. On the Parmelee bus. With the seats along the side."

"I sort of remember," Tootie said. "Go on."

"Well, you must remember Cousin Addie and the boys. We spent the night at their house."

"They had a little dog," Tootie said, "a little black dog. They didn't have a very big back yard."

"People in Chicago don't have big back yards," Agnes said. "They haven't as much room."

"I wouldn't like to live in Chicago," Tootie said. "I remember Grandma and Grandpa and the parrot."

"Well, I should think so! *They're* your relations."

Tootie was silent for a minute. Then she asked in a whisper, "Why is Grandpa blind?"

"He just got blind one day when he was twenty-seven years old," Agnes said.

"Oh," said Tootie. "He just got blind."

"You mustn't think about that, though," Agnes said. "You must think how lucky you are to be going on a train in the best seats, even changing cars in Chicago, and of how you can play all summer long with Bunchie Crocker on the beach or in the yard, and you can walk around in your bare feet."

"And I'm going to have my cemetery," Tootie said. "And a funeral every day. All my dolls are going to die, except Margaretha."

"Yes," Agnes said. "You'd better go to sleep now, Tootie."

In the next room, Mrs. Smith heard their voices and smiled. She had finished her packing, and she sat down in the small rocker and unbuttoned her dress at the neck. Her dark-brown hair was mussed, and she looked pretty as she sat there. For a few minutes she rocked gently back and forth, and then she got up and crossed the hall again, this time to Grandpa Prophater's room. She opened his door softly and listened. He was snoring gently.

ST. LOUIS *July 1903*

She closed his door and walked downstairs. Mr. Smith still sat in the chair near the window. "Well, Lonnie," she said. "The bed is cleared off now and you can go up."

He puffed at his cigar. "The girls finished?"

"*Almost*," she said.

"Lon?"

"Oh, he's probably asleep by now."

"Agnes and Tootie?"

"They're in bed, too," she said. "And so's Papa. He's been in bed since nine. You can go up now."

He put his arm around her waist and drew her closer. "How about playing a little something for me?" he said.

"Oh, Lonnie! I haven't played for ages. And I'll wake the children."

"If the noise that goes on here every night doesn't wake the children, nothing will," he said.

"Well—" She pulled away from him and walked out to the hall, where the piano stood. She twirled the stool before she sat down. Then she rubbed her hands together a few times and began to play. Mr. Smith stood beside her, his hand on her shoulder. She played softly and sang. Her voice was high. clear, and true.

Tootie, hearing the music, jumped out of bed and ran downstairs, and Rose and Esther opened the door of their room and hummed the tune. They heard Lon coming down the stairs from the third floor. "Are you going down?" Esther whispered to him as he passed. "Because if you're going down, we're going down."

Agnes lay in bed, listening to the music and thinking of what it would be like when they got to the depot at Manitowoc. First there would be Sheboygan and then there would be Manitowoc. There would be the ride in the carriage in the dusk over the brick streets, the different sound the horses' hoofs made when they crossed the bridge. And then there would be Grandma and Grandpa's house, and Grandma would be standing in the doorway with Polly perched on her shoulder. Agnes heard Esther and Rose and Lon as they tiptoed down the stairs, and she slid out of bed and followed them.

Mrs. Smith held Tootie in her lap, reaching around her to hit the piano keys. Rose, Esther,

ST. LOUIS *July 1903*

and Lon stood behind their mother with arms locked together. Agnes moved in close to her father and spoke. "'Erminie,'" she said.

Mrs. Smith smiled and nodded. "Bye, bye, drowsiness o'ertaking, Pretty little eyelids sleep," she sang.

Mr. Smith drew on his cigar once more before he threw it away. He looked at his children. It was after twelve o'clock, and their eyes were bright and shining. He knew that it would be another hour before the house was quiet for the night.

August 1903

AUGUST 1903

Rose Smith spread the cards face upward on the carpet. "Wait until I find myself," she said. She picked up the queen of clubs, set it aside, and then started to shuffle the rest of the pack. As she shuffled, she closed her eyes and frowned.

"Concentrate on your wish," her sister Esther said. "I know what it is, so I'll concentrate too." She covered her eyes with one hand, pressing the lids closed with her fingers.

The living room of Grandma Smith's house in Manitowoc, Wisconsin, was silent except for the faint rippling sound of the cards and the noise Polly made as she cracked open the seeds from her tin cup, which hung on one end of her perch.

"All right," Rose said finally. She laid the cards down again on the carpet and cut them in three piles, toward herself, with her left hand.

Esther leaned forward and turned the piles

over. "To the house comes a light-haired man," she said.

"A king of hearts," Rose said. "I should have thought the Colonel would be a king of diamonds. I mean he's not *really* blond, just brown-haired."

"Well, I'll admit I would have felt much better if you *had* cut the king of diamonds. But maybe his hair's turned darker with age. He *might* have been a heart once."

"I wish we knew how old he is," Rose said.

Esther smoothed her skirt thoughtfully. "Well, let's see," she said. "First off, he's a graduate of West Point and a colonel in the regular Army. And he went through the Spanish-American War."

"Oh, he's a real hero, all right," Rose agreed. She lifted her head proudly and let her eyelids droop. Esther noticed that the mere mention of the Colonel's past glories was enough to make Rose put on her most devastating expression.

"I think he's noticed you, I really do," Esther said.

Rose's laugh was affected. "My dear *enfant*," she said. "He doesn't even know I'm on earth."

"He saw you in your kimono," Esther reminded her.

Rose screamed politely at the recollection. "I hadn't any idea there was a soul in sight. And Mamma told me to call Tootie for lunch."

Although Esther knew every bit of the incident by heart, she asked, "And he came along with Snow?"

"With Snow," Rose repeated. "And he had that little stick he carries to manage Snow with. He looked just perfect. I didn't see him until he was nearly opposite the house, and then I ran in."

"And he laughed," Esther said. "And then knocked the leaves on the trees with his stick, so he *must* know you're alive."

"I wish we had a fancy breed dog," Rose sighed. "It seems to me we never have anything really exciting. Of course, Agnes has Lady Babbie, but she's pure, unadulterated *alley*. And poor Joe died. He was only part collie, anyway."

"He was a lovely animal," Esther said. She thought of Joe's broad, soft forehead and his melting eyes.

"I wish you'd been outdoors the evening Snow ran up and sniffed at me, and the Colonel said in a perfectly divine military voice, 'Here, Snow.'"

"I wish I had," Esther said. She selected twenty-one cards and dealt them out in piles of four around the queen of clubs, holding the odd card in her hand.

The screen door leading from the porch to the dining room opened and banged shut, and Tootie came into the room. Her hair was pinned in a knot on the top of her head, which gave her face a rather witchlike expression. She had stuck a piece of licorice gum over two of her upper front teeth and in one hand she carried an old medicine bottle filled with a pinkish-colored liquid. She paused at the door to the living room and, lifting the bottle to her lips, took a large swallow.

"Go away, Tootie," Esther said. "We're busy."

"I've been having a wake," Tootie said. "A real Irish wake like Katie told me about." The gum in her mouth made her speak indistinctly. "Maude Rockerfeller died this morning, and Bunchie and I buried her. She was one of the richest dolls, so we put her by herself nearest the little pond. Her leg came off and she bled to death. She bled to death in about a second."

"Her leg *came* off," Rose said. "It *came* off, all right. *I* saw you throwing her in the air and not even trying to catch her."

"I caught her twice," Tootie said. "And I wasn't throwing her. She had a raging fever and she was out of her head. She was *jumping*. It was all I could do to hang on to her. And the third time, she fell and hit the pavement and bled to death. We put her in her coffin and stood it on end and made a clay pipe out of a piece of clover and stuck it in her mouth. Katie says that's what they always do. It was a real wake, and the best funeral we've ever had."

She lifted the bottle to her mouth and took another swallow. "Consumption has no pity for blue eyes and golden hair," she sang.

"What's that stuff you're swilling?" Esther asked.

Tootie held the bottle up to the light. "Well," she said, "it's a little bit of everything. We got a few raspberries that were left, and some lemon juice. And we squeezed some sour grass and a whole peach, and the rest is rain water. It was part of the refreshments. *After*, you know."

"Well, go away and play with Bunchie some more," Rose said.

"All right," Tootie said. "I just wanted to say that the Colonel spoke to us."

Rose fell backward on the floor. Her soft, dark-brown pompadour parted in the middle and her side combs slipped out. *"Nom de Dieu!"* she exclaimed.

Esther stood up and grasped Tootie firmly by the shoulders. "Now, Tootie, if you're making up things again, I'll *really* shake you till your teeth rattle."

"It's true," Tootie said. "We were just sprinkling the dirt over Maude's coffin when he spoke to us. He was in that buggy of his—"

"Buggy!" Rose moaned. "Buggy! It's a trap. A dear little trap. Go on!"

"And he stopped," Tootie went on. "And when he stopped, that horse of his—"

"Tootie!" Esther's voice was stern.

"I was merely going to say that maybe he didn't mean to stop. Maybe the horse—"

"That is neither here nor there," Rose said. "What did he *say*?"

ST. LOUIS *August 1903*

"He said hello. And we said hello back. And then he asked what we were doing and we told him. So then he said he was sorry. There was another man with him."

Rose sat up and looked meaningly at Esther. "How old was *he?*"

"He was old, too. He had one leg."

"Wounded!" Rose said. "Wounded in the war!"

Tootie looked disappointed. "I thought maybe a train ran over him," she said. "Like Jake Harvey. A train ran over him the time he rolled down onto the tracks when he was drunk."

"Wouldn't it be divine if the Colonel had gotten wounded too?" Esther asked.

"Well, it's not the Colonel's fault he wasn't wounded so it would show and excite sympathy. Go *on*, Tootie."

"That's all," Tootie said.

"It couldn't be all," Rose said. "Did he look up at the house, or even mention our names?"

Tootie frowned. "I don't think he did. He called the man Captain something, and he said, 'Captain something, this is one of the little Smith girls.' And the Captain said, 'You don't say. How many of them are there?' And the Colonel said, 'There are four and not a lemon in the bunch.'"

"Did you hear that, Ess?" Rose asked. "I ask you, did you hear it?"

"Then Agnes came by with Bunchie's sister," Tootie went on. "They were going down to ride on the bridge, and we wanted to go. We wanted to see the Père Marquette. But she and Bunchie wouldn't take us. She lifted her eyebrows and looked right through the Colonel and that other man."

"Mamma's got to stop Agnes doing that," Rose said. "She just can't go around looking through people and giving them the wrong impression of us all."

Esther had buried her face in her hands, and now she looked up, her cheeks flushed and her black eyes shining. "Listen, Tootie," she said. "Will you do something? Will you see if Grandma or Mamma are in the kitchen, or Mamie?" Mamie was Grandma Smith's hired girl.

"I won't have to," Tootie said. "Grandma and Mamma went to the jeweler's. They took

ST. LOUIS *August 1903*

Grandpa with them. He didn't want to go, but they thought the air would do him good. Mamma had some settings loose in her rings. And Mamie's down by the back gate picking beans."

"That's wonderful," Esther said. "Well, there are some chicken hearts in a big bowl all mixed up with the rest of the chicken. I saw them this morning. And you get two and bring them in here."

"Chicken hearts!" Rose exclaimed. "Ess, you are absolutely fiendish. Do you think we dare? Suppose Jewett Ottmar shows up, or Chet Murphy?"

"We'll just have to crawfish out of shaking hands with them," Esther said. "Because if I ever swallowed a chicken heart whole and had to shake hands with either of them, you'd have to call the hurry-up wagon."

"Would you die?" Tootie asked.

Rose and Esther screamed with laughter. "Almost," Rose said. "Only worse. When you swallow a chicken heart you have to marry the first man you shake hands with."

"Oh," Tootie said. She turned and walked toward the door. "I'll get them, but I'm going to stay and watch. If it works, can I have some of your old ribbons for dolls' dresses?"

"If it works, you can have *anything*," Rose said.

"Of course, I've never seen the Captain," Esther said. "For all we know, he might be a perfect pill. Although I don't think the Colonel would know a pill."

Rose was pleased that Esther had made no trouble about the Colonel. It would have been dreadful if she had wanted to shake hands with him first. "The Captain's probably perfectly sweet," she said. "And with only one leg, too. He probably has a trunk full of medals. You could do lots worse. Just think, Mr. Gregory won't even graduate from West Point for two more years, and even then he'll only be a second lieutenant."

"He'll be at the Fair in St. Louis next summer, though," Esther said. "And we'll be at home at 5135, because we can't come to Manitowoc when there's a fair. And I certainly won't be married by then."

"Of course you won't, *enfant*," Rose said. "You're too young to get married. But it will be nice to *know*. I'll be glad *knowing*. Once I *know*, I can do anything I like, just the same as now. Only I won't have to worry about anything. Fate helps."

Tootie came back into the room carrying a plate on which she had put the two raw chicken hearts. "Here they are," she said.

The hearts looked red and unappetizing, but Rose stepped forward and picked one up. "Here goes," she said. She shut her eyes. "I vow solemnly that I will marry the next man I shake hands with." She popped the heart in her mouth and swallowed quickly.

Esther's eyes grew wide. "You did it," she said. "You did it. I never saw anything so calm in my life." She picked the other heart from the plate and shuddered. "I hope I can swallow it. You know how I was with that capsule."

"Don't think about it," Rose said. "Just do it."

Esther opened her mouth, gagging a little as she placed the heart far back on her tongue. She swallowed hard and choked. "It's not all the way down," she said. "It feels like a lump."

"That'll go away," Tootie assured her. "I swallowed an all-day sucker once, and it went away after about an hour."

There were footsteps on the porch, and through the living-room window the girls could see their brother Lon. He had been swimming in Lake Michigan and his hair was damp and slicked back on his head. He hung his bathing suit over the railing and came into the house. "Oh, here you are," he said to Tootie.

Esther pinched Tootie's shoulder hard. "If you tell him what we've done—" she warned.

"Esther didn't take the oath," Tootie said. "Rose took it, but Esther didn't."

"It doesn't matter," Rose said hurriedly. "She thought it."

"Tootie," Lon said, "as I was coming up the path to the house, I just happened to look over at your cemetery."

"Oh, yes," Tootie said. "Bunchie and I had a funeral today."

Lon closed his eyes, tilted his head back, and pursed his lips thoughtfully. "That's it, then," he said. "That's what I heard." An expression of horror burst over his face. "Oh, my God!"

"What is it? What is it, Lon?" Tootie asked. "Grave-robbers?"

"Grave-robbers!" Lon exclaimed. "If it were only that!" He buried his face in his hands and his shoulders shook. "I can't tell you, Tootie. I haven't the nerve."

Tootie set the plate down on the round mahogany table and ran over to him and pulled at his coat violently. "What is it?" she cried.

Lon uncovered his face and struggled to compose his features. "A living death," he said.

Tootie looked at him sharply. "Maude was dead when we buried her," she said. "She didn't make a sound or move a finger all the time we were fixing her in her shroud. And we had a long ceremony, too."

Lon sighed with relief. "Well, it's all right then. I expect that sound I heard, that moaning sound, was just the wind."

"A moaning sound?" Tootie asked.

"It was quite loud," Lon said. "It sounded like a soul in agony. Tell me, Tootie, what position was she in when you put her in the coffin?"

"Flat on her back, of course," Tootie said. "What do you suppose?"

"Well, I'd dig her up and give her a look, anyway. If she's still on her back, I wouldn't worry about her. But if she's moved—"

Tootie's face was stricken. Suddenly she began to scream. "She's alive! She's alive and suffocating!" She turned and ran from the room.

Esther, Rose, and Lon heard the screen door bang and the sound of Tootie's sandals as she ran across the porch and down the path. "Bunchie! Bunchie!" she called. "Get a spoon quick! We've got to dig up Maude."

Lon turned to the girls and brushed some dirt from his hands. "What was on the plate?" he asked.

"Just something for Polly," Rose answered. "Come on, Ess, let's sit under the big tree near the street."

"We'll get our skirts grass-stained," Esther said. She looked at Rose meaningly. "You can see the street *plainly* from the porch. I've always noticed when I've been going by the house how easy it is to see up on the porch, too."

Rose straightened her hair and put her arm around Esther's waist. "It's too hot inside," she said.

"Wait until I get a glass of water," Lon said, "and I'll be with you."

"Chet came by looking for you after you went to the beach," Esther said. "I think he wanted you to come over."

"I just saw him," Lon said. "He's coming here."

Rose gasped. "No," she said. "He can't come over here."

"Like H he can't," Lon said. He went into the kitchen and they could hear the sound of the pump handle as he worked it up and down.

The two girls walked slowly out onto the porch. It was hot in the sun, but there was a cool breeze from the lake. The side porch was large and shady because of the vines that covered it, but they moved two wicker rocking chairs to the front of the porch, where they could be seen from the street. The air was sweet with the scent of sweet peas, and they could see across the flower garden and the vegetable garden as far as the back gate that led to the barn. The tassels on the corn had turned brown in the sun, and along the path that ran from the front steps to the street the peony bushes drooped in the heat. Mamie's blue dress and white apron showed as she moved among the vines, which were heavy with beans. At the far end of the flower garden Tootie and Bunchie were digging frantically.

Lon came out of the house and strolled to the front of the porch, where he sat on the railing. "I should think you'd want to sit around the side," he said. "It's hot here."

"You may sit where you want," Rose answered. "We prefer it here. No one wants to sit on a side porch where they can't see anything but a lot of trees and some outhouses."

Lon looked at Tootie and Bunchie and smiled. "I'd just as soon sit here," he said.

Far up the street the sound of a horse's hoofs could be heard. "Not fast enough," Rose said, turning to Esther, who glanced at her anxiously. "I must say I do like a spirited horse."

They watched idly as old Mr. Meade

drove by in his surrey. "The Meades' surrey is just plain tacky," Esther said.

"Here they come," Lon said.

"*Who* do you mean by *they*?" Rose asked. She pulled her skirts out so that they hung full at the side and swept the floor.

"Chet Murphy and Frank Gregory."

The two girls sprang to their feet and stared at each other in anguish. "What'll we do?" Esther asked. "You've got to think of something." She clasped her hands behind her back. "I won't! I can't!"

"Begin to pick flowers or something quick!" Rose cried. She ran down the porch steps and pulled at the faded peony bushes. Esther stood paralyzed, her hands clenched. She saw that Chet Murphy and Frank Gregory had already started up the path, and she saw to her horror that Rose had safely filled her hands with the dried stalks of the peony bushes.

"Working on this hot day?" Chet Murphy asked.

Rose looked up and smiled at him. Her face was calm and the poise of her head was dignified. Frank Gregory spoke to her and hurried up the steps. "Well, Miss Esther!" he exclaimed, and held out his hand.

Esther stared at him wildly. "No!" she said. "I can't! Go away, Mr. Gregory. Go away, I'm warning you!"

The young man looked straight into her eyes, and she saw that his were very blue. She closed her eyes, murmuring weakly, "No!"

"Why, Miss Esther," he said. "Have I done something wrong? If I have, I'm sorry."

At the sound of his voice something inside her weakened. She thought of the Captain, whom she had never seen and who was probably as old as the Colonel. And she thought of next summer, when all of the cadets would be coming to St. Louis for the Fair. Most of all, she thought of the way Frank Gregory had looked standing there. Without opening her eyes, she unclasped her hands and held the right one out. He took it and shook it firmly. Her lids opened slowly, and the dimples showed in her cheeks. "Well, don't say you weren't *warned*," she said.

They walked to the top step and sat down side by side. Rose could hear them talking softly together, and she wondered if Esther

ST. LOUIS *August 1903*

were telling him about the chicken hearts. She walked past them up the steps and Chet Murphy followed her. Putting the dried stalks of the peonies at the side of the porch, she brushed her hands together daintily and sat down. Chet Murphy sat at her feet.

Tootie came slowly up the path, her walk triumphant. She stood in the grass, looking up at Lon. "You were right," she said. "We opened up the grave, and there she was in her coffin *on her side*. She was unconscious. And just when I was trying to revive her, she must have slipped off the rock where we'd laid her out, and she hit another rock. Her head's off now. And I don't think a person with her head off could be alive. Do you?"

Lon began to laugh. "Darned if I do!" he said. He fished in his pocket and took out a nickel, which he tossed to her. She caught it expertly with a long-practiced gesture.

"Oh, thanks," she said. "Thanks a whole lot. We can get ten tiny dolls for this. The tiny dolls are plenty good enough—" She paused and turned her head so that she could see the dolls' cemetery with its small lake the size of a kitchen bowl. "Thanks," she said again, and skipped down the path to where Bunchie stood waiting.

The Colonel and his friend the Captain drove by almost before Rose could get a glimpse of them. They glanced up at the porch. The trap was painted black and yellow and it was very smart, while between the two men, Snow, the English bull terrier, sat proudly. Rose sighed. "That's a beautiful horse," she said. "And a perfectly darling trap."

"Oh, the horse is all right. And the trap's all right, I guess," Chet Murphy said. "But the two men in it—well, they're not all right."

"They are heroes," Rose told him proudly. "And I think they bring a little excitement to Manitowoc. Heaven knows it needs it. I think it's just wonderful to see the Colonel going to the grocery store every morning for bread and things. Somehow or other one never associates soldiers and football players, for instance, with anything the least domestic. I think it's thrilling to see them doing such tame things as buy bread, or mail letters, or do things like other everyday people."

"I guess they're everyday enough," Chet

Murphy said. "Because Mother asked around about them and there is some doubt that the Colonel is a colonel. He used to live in Milwaukee and some friends of Mother's said he had the rep of being pretty frisky. Almost fast. At least his capacity for mixed drinks is said to be unlimited. I know he doesn't do a stroke of work."

"Isn't even a colonel?" Rose asked. Her face grew stern. "Well, I must say, I don't think it very noble of him to go around deceiving people."

Chet Murphy, seeing the expression in her eyes, grew red. "I didn't say he *wasn't* a colonel," he said. "He may have been once for all I know. After all, he's almost forty."

"Almost forty," Rose repeated. "Well, Esther and I have had a lot of fun over the poor old thing. He really makes us laugh at times, the way he stares so fiercely at us and always pulls his cuffs down and straightens up when we pass by."

She glanced down the street, and there was a faraway look in her eyes. Esther and Frank Gregory were still laughing and talking and Lon was smoking his pipe. Chet Murphy sat still, his hands clasping his knees. Rose shook her head impatiently. After all, she thought, Chet was there and he had come to call. It was only polite to be nice to him. Besides, she remembered, he had once told her he admired her handwriting. She turned her head until she was looking at him out of the corner of her eyes. He was better than nothing.

He heard the rustle of her dress as she moved and saw that she was smiling. It seemed to him he had never seen anyone as beautiful or as kind.

September 1903

SEPTEMBER 1903

Agnes Smith ran along the sidewalk under the maple trees. Even in her excitement she did not forget to hit each tree as she passed with a small, leafy branch that she held in her hand. Her face was flushed, and her hair, which was parted in the middle and braided into two pigtails caught up and tied together by a wide plaid ribbon, swayed from side to side as she ran. She was too big to wear socks, her mother thought, and now the seams of her black ribbed stockings were crooked on her slim legs. Her movements were swift and graceful. When she came to the terrace of 5135 Kensington Avenue, she turned and climbed up the slippery, dry grass and, speeding up now that she was near her goal, she cut across the lawn to the back porch. As her foot hit the first step, she cried out, "Mamma! Mamma!"

The kitchen of the Smiths' house was very hot. The air was pungent and sweet with the smell from a large kettle of chili sauce that simmered on the back of the old coal stove. As Agnes called, Mrs. Smith lifted a wooden spoon to her lips and tasted the mixture judicially. "I think I've got it a little too sweet," she said to Katie.

"I hear Agnes," Katie said.

Agnes opened the screen door and stood looking at the two women. Her gray eyes shone and she wiped her forehead daintily with one hand. "Mamma!" she repeated. "Guess what."

"Your mother has no time for guessing," Katie said sternly. She walked across the kitchen and pulled the bow tighter on Agnes' braids.

"You'll *never* guess," Agnes said.

Mrs. Smith put down the spoon so that it rested across the sides of the kettle. "Well, tell me and get it over with, then. But if you're going to tattle on your sisters—"

"I'm not interested in my sisters," Agnes said. "What I was going to say was merely that I *almost* saw Mrs. Johnson."

"No!" her mother exclaimed.

"You're sure you're telling the truth, now?" Katie asked, eying her suspiciously.

"Cross my heart and hope to die on the spot," Agnes said. She sat down in the big rocking chair and rocked back and forth solemnly. "I'd been to the corner to see if the mud puddle was as big as it was yesterday, and it wasn't. So then I was coming back home, just walking and not doing anything particular. And when I got in front of the Johnsons' house I looked up, and that's when I almost saw Mrs. Johnson."

"What was she doing?" Mrs. Smith asked.

"I don't know," Agnes said. "The lace curtains sort of moved and I could see part of her hand. So I thought I'd better tell you."

"I'd like to see the inside of that house," Katie said, "with her always sitting in front of that window with her eyes peeled on the street. It's a month since she moved in; the place must be an inch thick with dust."

"Oh, it's neat enough," Mrs. Smith said. "By that I mean that the furniture in the hall looks all right. Of course, I only saw it out of the corner of my eye when Mr. Johnson let himself in with his key."

"You can be neat and not clean," Katie said flatly.

"Well, he's a wonderful man," Mrs. Smith said. "I don't know how he puts up with her. Every night I see him coming down the street with a parcel in his hand. I must say it puzzled me until one time I saw the brown paper was stained with blood, so I assumed it must be a small steak for their dinner."

"Can you beat that, now?" Katie murmured.

Mrs. Smith smoothed her apron and looked more brisk and efficient than usual. "Well, everyone to his taste, as the old lady said when she kissed the cow, so for all I know, Mr. Johnson doesn't mind. But I must say that a woman can't be much of a woman when she's too lazy to do her own marketing."

Katie looked at her shrewdly. "And it may be that he's too stingy," she said. "The sort that watches things."

"Never!" Mrs. Smith exclaimed. "Never in this world! Why, look at the shape of his mouth. You never saw a man with a mouth shaped like that who was stingy, did you? And look at the way their lawn is kept. Perfect! You don't get a lawn like that without spending some money on it."

"He's a nice-looking man," Katie said.

Mrs. Smith took out her back comb and caught up the fine curls that had worked themselves loose. "He's a very handsome man," she said. "I don't think I ever saw such a *black* mustache."

The door from the back hall opened and Rose came into the kitchen. "Oh," she said. "I thought you'd be through. I thought I'd make some coconut haystacks to send to Lon. Who has a black mustache?"

"Mr. Johnson," Katie answered.

Rose leaned languidly against the door of the kitchen closet and looked down at her nails, which were pink and shining. "I don't believe I could be civil to anyone with a mustache," she said.

"No one's asked you to," her mother said. "What have you been doing to your nails?"

"Esther and I bought a lot of manicure articles and we fixed our nails. While I did mine, Ess read to me. And when she did hers, I read to her. We were reading 'Wanted, a Matchmaker.'"

Katie snorted. "Reading!" she said. "And

your mother worn to the bone making preserves. And neither of you helping. And not once did you offer to help mark your own brother's clothes before he went away."

"We did offer to," Rose said, "but Mamma didn't want us fooling with the indelible ink. We made him a big box of fudge and stuffed a lot of apples in his trunk so that he'd be sure to have something to eat his first day there."

"Yes, I can imagine!" Katie said. "I can imagine that in a big place like Princeton they haven't a crust of bread to hand out to their students. I can imagine that he would have starved to death by now if it hadn't been for the fudge."

"And we weren't only reading," Rose went on, unperturbed. "We were trying to decide something. We weren't going to tell you, Mamma, but I'm afraid we're going to have to."

Mrs. Smith lifted Agnes up from the rocker and sat down on it herself, pulling Agnes onto her lap. Agnes' head drooped toward her mother's cheek. Slight as the movement was, Mrs. Smith felt it and held Agnes closer in her arms. She noticed that Agnes was wearing another one of the Peter Thomson suits that had once belonged to Esther. It was hard to be twelve, she thought, and have a sister whose clothes had to be made to fit because they were too good to be thrown away.

"We're going to have to," Rose repeated.

"What's happened now?" her mother asked sharply. She rocked the chair vigorously.

"It's Lon," Rose said.

"Lon?"

"Yes," Rose went on. "I got a letter from him on the four-o'clock delivery. It wasn't a letter exactly; it was more of a note. He simply wants us to speak to Papa. He enclosed his weekly account."

"Well," Mrs. Smith said, "give it to your father when he comes home."

Rose polished her nails against her blouse. "I don't think we'd better. You see, practically the minute he left town, Lon spent his whole allowance. All of it."

"But he's only been there a week and that money was to last him through October," Mrs. Smith said.

"I know," Rose said calmly. "Esther and

I went over it time after time. We couldn't think of anything to do, so we simply began to read Paul Leicester Ford out loud. Of course, we wouldn't have said anything about it to you, but we didn't have any money to send him ourselves. Not enough, anyway. You see, we'd bought the manicure articles *before* we got the letter."

Mrs. Smith stopped rocking and stared out through the screen door to the back porch. From where she sat, she could see the patch on the screen and the pool on the porch floor where the icebox leaked. The water, standing all summer on the floor, had blistered the paint. She reached up and smoothed Agnes' hair with her hand. Her fingers were rough and caught in the fine hair. Her shoulders ached, and she remembered that she and Katie had scalded and peeled three bushels of tomatoes that day, besides peeling and chopping dozens of onions and green peppers. She looked up at the kitchen clock, saw that it was after half past five, and was dimly aware that Katie had just started to prepare dinner. And then her mind wandered unaccountably to Mrs. Johnson, a woman she had never seen, a woman who apparently sat all day in her parlor, one pale hand resting on her expensive lace curtains so that she could pull them aside an inch or so when she heard footsteps on the street. She thought of Mr. Johnson and the way he looked as he walked by the Smith house every evening, and it seemed to her that he carried his brown paper bundle almost proudly home to a wife who was too fine and too beloved to be annoyed with the everyday things of life. She jumped up from the chair and Agnes slid to the floor. "I've had all the nonsense I'm going to stand!" she cried. "Where's that letter? Go get me that letter! What did he spend all that money on?"

Rose's eyes were frightened. "On a smoking and shaving outfit," she answered.

"A smoking and shaving outfit! When he knows your father has your school bill and Esther's school bill to worry him!"

"I should say so!" Agnes said from the floor. "All those school bills. I must say I'm glad I go to public school."

"That'll be enough from you, Miss!" her mother said. "Your time is coming. It'll be private school next year for you too. And take the smug look off your face before I box your ears! And you, Katie, stop standing there and get busy with that dinner!" She flounced past Rose, who followed her meekly out of the room.

Katie turned to Agnes, who still lay on the floor. "Your mother can sure make the fur fly when she sets her mind to it," she said proudly. "I don't think I ever knew a woman with as quick a temper."

Agnes picked herself up with dignity. "I think I'll listen to the fight," she said. She walked slowly out of the kitchen and up the back stairs. The door to the room that Esther and Rose shared was closed, but she could hear voices plainly, her mother's loudest of all. She sat down on the top step and took a hard gumdrop from her pocket and put it in her mouth. Then she settled her chin comfortably in the palms of her hands.

In the bedroom, Mrs. Smith stood with her back to the window, facing the two girls. The manicure set lay upset on the floor, where she had kicked it. Esther's black eyes were defiant. "If you'll let us get a word in—" she said.

"Get a word in! I'd like to know the time when either of you ever had trouble getting a word in! No, Rose! And I'll say it to your face. You've made a fool of your brother with your talk over the telephone to your friends. *'Mon frère à* Princeton!'" She snorted. "No wonder he's gone hog-wild and spent all his money. He probably thinks nothing's too good for him now. And the way you came home from the station, your eyes as red as beets."

At the thought of the parting scene at the Union Station, Esther's eyes filled dramatically with tears. "If you could have *seen* him when he got on the train," she said. "With his little cap, and his long overcoat, and his grand, baggy pants."

"He looked absolutely keen," Rose said. "And he went with a whole lot of Princeton men who were going back. Seniors! They said they were going to show him all over Princeton."

"And I suppose your hearts were broken," Mrs. Smith said. "But they weren't so broken that you couldn't find your way to Plow's and eat two sundaes apiece." She turned and stared out of the window. The sun was low and the huge maple trees in front of the house cast dark shadows across the street, which was damp where the water wagon had sprinkled it lightly.

"Lon wrote that he got a cinder in his eye, too," Rose said. "It stayed in three days and the pain was excruciating."

"It's too bad it didn't blind him," Mrs. Smith answered shortly. "Then he wouldn't have been able to pick out a fine shaving and smoking outfit."

"*I'll* tell Papa," Rose said.

Mrs. Smith turned to face the two girls again. "You'll do nothing of the sort. Heaven only knows what your father will do. Do you want your brother brought home from college in disgrace?"

"We could take the manicure articles back," Esther said. "But the buffer shows where it's been used."

The two girls looked at their mother anxiously. She was calmer, and their eyes were hopeful.

"I mean I'd just as soon eat fish all week if that would help," Esther said. "I mean it isn't utterly necessary to have roast beef for Sunday."

"Well," Mrs. Smith said. "You see, it's like this. For one thing, there's no use talking to your father. Not about Lon. I can handle him when it comes to you girls, but I can't do a thing with him about Lon. Now, if we could get a little money together this week, and a little next week, and so on until his next allowance is due, we might patch it up without your father getting wind of it."

From down the street there was the sound of footsteps. Mrs. Smith stepped back from the window and peered out through the curtains. "It's Mr. Johnson," she said. "And he's got his package the same as usual. Now, *there's* a woman who leads the life of Riley."

Rose walked over to the window. "He *is* handsome," she said. "Even with that mustache. I wonder what he's got in that bag."

"His dinner, poor soul," her mother answered. "He brings it home with him every night so that *she* won't have to soil her hands carrying it. It wouldn't surprise me if he cooked it for her, too."

Esther's eyes grew round with amazement. "Oh, she couldn't let him do *that*!"

"I wouldn't put it past her," Mrs. Smith

said. "I've been watching him every night since we came home from vacation. And it's a well-known fact that she never turns a wheel. Mrs. Wagner saw her once, and she told me that she's never seen anything to beat her. Went along the street as though she were walking on eggs."

"Maybe they're poor and he markets downtown because it's cheaper," Esther said. "After all, they don't own that house. Just rent it. I certainly would hate to live in a rented house."

Mrs. Smith shook her head. "He's probably living in it a while to see how he likes it. It would be the sensible thing to do. Your father and I rented this house for two months before we bought it." She watched Mr. Johnson's back until he turned to walk up the steps of his house, and then she sighed. "I don't know when I've ever seen a man with such a kind, understanding face," she said. "I should imagine everyone who knows him goes to him with their troubles."

"A man like that would be nice," Rose said.

"Yes," her mother agreed. "A man like that would be a great change. A great change.

ST. LOUIS *September 1903*

Well, my mother always told me never to marry a man I had to handle, but I didn't heed her advice. I thought I knew it all, just as you, Rose, think you know it all." She walked over and opened the door. "Well, Big Ears," she said. "I suppose you've heard every word."

Agnes got up from the top step and smoothed her skirts. "I have a dollar," she said. "I've been saving it, but you can have it for a while. Then when Lon gets caught up, he can send it back to me." She frowned thoughtfully. "With some interest."

"I wonder if your grandfather has a little tucked away somewhere," Mrs. Smith said.

"I'm not sure," Agnes said. "But Tootie has a quarter. At least, she had a quarter when she started out this afternoon."

"Well, now, I'll tell you what," Mrs. Smith said. "We'll get as much together as we can *now*. And we'll eat light for a while. If there are any questions from your father or Grandpa, we'll say we think it's too hot for big, heavy meals." She began to smile and, turning to Agnes, she winked slightly.

There was tension at the dinner table that night and an undercurrent of excitement.

Tootie, who sat at the foot of the table next to her mother, pushed her food thoughtfully around her plate. "That man on the water sprinkler is *little*," she said. "He's about as big as a dwarf. I rode as far as Delmar with him, and he brought me all the way back."

Rose lifted her eyebrows. "It's mean to remark on the imperfections in the looks of others. It is just like telling or hinting to the Lord that you could have done the job up better if it had been left to you."

Grandpa Prophater gave her a quick, keen glance. His eyes were like jet. "The Queen," he said. "The Queen speaks."

"Lonnie," Mrs. Smith said, "did you go down to work on the same trolley as Mr. Johnson? I noticed he left the house just after you. So I wondered if you happened to catch the same trolley."

"Johnson?" Mr. Smith asked. "The fellow who's just moved in down the street?"

"The Johnsons have lived there over a month," his wife told him, and her voice was patient.

"Mamma thinks Mr. Johnson is a fine-looking man," Agnes said. "So do I."

"I don't like Mrs. Johnson." Tootie shook

her head so violently that her chair creaked. "She told me not to run across their lawn. When Halloween comes, I'm going to get even with her."

Mrs. Smith turned toward Tootie and stared at her in amazement. "You mean you've actually talked to her? Why didn't you say so? What does she look like? And what did she say?"

"I've talked to her a thousand times," Tootie answered. "Every time I run over her lawn I talk to her. She has a daughter named Mamie, and she's away at college. Mrs. Johnson says that she wishes I wouldn't run over her lawn, and I don't say anything much. I just say the lawn isn't hers, it belongs to Mr. Yule, and she only rents it from Mr. Yule. So then once she said she had the care of it. She doesn't like me. She practically told me so. She called me a hoodlum."

"You *are* a hoodlum," her mother said. "Did you hear that, Lonnie? Mr. Johnson has a daughter who is away at college. I just know that girl has *everything*. Probably clothes like a princess and spending money galore." She cut the crust of her pie. "There's a great deal to be said for having only *one* child."

Tootie's fork clattered to the floor and Agnes pushed back her chair and ran from the room. Rose and Esther looked at their mother as though she were demented.

"Anna!" Grandpa Prophater said sternly.

Mr. Smith pushed back his plate and folded his napkin. "Why, Anna!" he said.

Mrs. Smith's eyes filled with tears. "Well, there is," she insisted. "When you have *one* child, you can do something for it. You don't have to wonder and wonder and wonder all the time."

Rose got up from the table and stood with her hand on her father's shoulder. "Just the same, Mamma, it's a dreadful thing to say. You can imagine how *we* feel with you wishing we were all dead."

Mr. Smith took Rose's hand and put it gently aside. "Agnes!" he called. "Come back here! Rose, sit down in your chair, where you belong. I have a few words to say."

The portières that hung in the doorway that led into the living room parted and Agnes came silently back to her place at the table. Mr. Smith looked around at the faces of his daughters and then at the flushed face of his wife. He cleared his throat. "Your mother," he said to the girls, "does not wish you were dead. What worries your mother is that she wants to give you heaven and earth. If she had the earth in her hands, she would divide it amongst you. Your mother was an only child, and the prettiest girl I ever saw. She could sing, too. Now she doesn't sing much any more, but she's the best damned cook in the state."

"Lonnie," Mrs. Smith murmured, "you don't have to swear."

"She could dance too," Mr. Smith went on. "Why, when I first married your mother, she could kick my hat off."

The girls turned and stared at their mother. She was smiling. "That was the time Corinne Archambault and I had the sherry," she said.

"Now," Mr. Smith said, "something's happened to upset your mother. I don't know what it is, but something's upset her."

"It's nothing," Mrs. Smith interrupted hurriedly. "It's nothing at all, is it, girls? I suppose it was foolish of me, but I got to thinking that if any emergency did arise, why, do you know, the most money I could raise would be about five dollars? And that's even counting in some of the house money."

September 1903

The door to the kitchen opened and Katie came into the room. She coughed and held up three fingers. "Eight dollars," she said.

Grandpa Prophater looked at his daughter from under his eyebrows. His hand slid into his pocket and he brought out a five-dollar bill. "Thirteen," he said.

Mr. Smith fumbled in his coat and took out his wallet. He placed a ten-dollar bill on the table. "Twenty-three," he said.

Tootie began to laugh wildly. "Twenty-three, skiddoo!" she screamed. "Twenty-three, skiddoo!"

Mr. Smith pulled his chair closer to the table, unfolded his napkin, and began to eat his pie again. "Now that *that's* over," he said, "what were we talking about?"

"We were talking about the Johnsons," Agnes said.

"Oh, yes." Mr. Smith chewed his mouthful of pie slowly. "I did get on the same trolley with Johnson this morning. As a matter of fact, I sat in the same seat with him." He wiped his mouth and pushed his plate back on the table. "Johnson," he said, "dyes his mustache."

October 1903

OCTOBER 1903

Agnes and Tootie had hurried through their dinner and now stood in front of the asbestos gas grate in their room. They were in their underwear, and although their legs burned with the heat of the flames, their backs were chilly. Tootie held a piece of ruled paper in her hands and looked at it thoughtfully. On the page was a picture of a black cat and under it the word "BEWARE" was printed in heavy black pencil. "I wonder who could have done it," Tootie said.

Agnes' gray eyes were scornful. She straightened her thin little shoulders and turned around to warm her back. "I'd ignore it," she said. "Probably Grandpa did it. Or the girls."

"But it wasn't *inside* the house," Tootie said. "It was slipped under the front door. And I asked Grandpa and Rose and Esther, and they swore they'd never laid eyes on it before."

"Papa, then," Agnes said.

"Papa can't draw. At least, he can only draw men in derby hats. He can't draw cats. I've never known him to." Tootie fidgeted nervously. "Besides, there was that letter."

Agnes laughed shrilly. "That letter!" she repeated. "That letter, if you noticed, was postmarked 'Princeton, New Jersey.' It was from Lon."

"It never was!" Tootie cried. "At least, I couldn't see that it was postmarked 'Princeton.' And inside it was marked 'Holyrood Cemetery,' *and* signed 'Peter Stuyvesant, deceased.' You know what 'deceased' means, don't you? It means 'dead'!" She stared at the fire, at the yellow flame edged with blue, until her eyes grew fixed.

"Even if it wasn't in Lon's handwriting, it was from Lon, all right," Agnes said. "You ought to know your own brother by now. He's always going on about banshees, and there were banshees in that letter. And even if it isn't from Lon and banshees are going to meet us down by the ashpit, we don't have to meet *them*."

Tootie clutched at her sister's arm. "What was that?"

They listened. Somewhere in the distance they heard the sound of moans. As the moans grew louder, they faced each other, their eyes wide and startled.

"It's from down by the ashpit," Tootie said in a whisper.

They stood, scarcely breathing, until they heard their mother's steps in the upstairs hall. Tootie loosed her clutch on Agnes' arms as Mrs. Smith entered the room. She carried two pairs of Lon's pajamas over her arm, and she smiled comfortingly.

"Here we are," she said.

They looked at her solemnly. "Where are Rose and Esther?" Tootie asked.

"Rose and Esther?" Their mother's voice was casual. "Why, they're downstairs in the parlor, I believe."

"Where's Papa?" Agnes asked.

"Playing solitaire." Mrs. Smith unfolded the pajamas and held them toward the fire to warm them.

"Where's Grandpa?" Tootie drew closer to her mother and waited anxiously for her reply.

"In his room burning some cork for your

hands. And Katie is washing the dinner dishes. What *has* got into you?"

Another moan came from out of the darkness, a moan that ended in a shriek.

"Well," Tootie said, "what a funny noise!"

"What *are* you talking about?" Mrs. Smith asked. "I didn't hear any funny noise. I can hear the trolley at the corner, but I wouldn't call that a funny noise."

Agnes laughed. "Oh, Tootie thinks there are banshees down by the ashpit, like it said in that letter from Lon," she said. "At least, it must have been from Lon, because it was postmarked 'Princeton.'"

Mrs. Smith frowned and shook her head. "That's strange," she said. "I never thought."

"Never thought what?" Tootie asked.

"Why, never thought that Lon isn't at Princeton. He wrote me three or four days ago that he was going to New York for a little visit. I suppose I forgot to mention it to you." Mrs. Smith shook the trousers of one pair of pajamas and stooped down, holding it so that Tootie could step into the legs.

Tootie put her legs into the pajama pants automatically.

ST. LOUIS *October 1903*

"Be careful and don't run over Mrs. Wagner's lawn," Mrs. Smith said. "It's covered with manure."

"We never run over her lawn," Agnes said. "She's nice. We're going to run over Mrs. Johnson's lawn, and we're going to carry away her bench and doormat if she hasn't put them away. We're going to absolutely wreck the Waughops', aren't we, Tootie?"

Tootie fastened the pajamas tightly around her waist. "I'm going to do a lot of things," she said. "There's no telling what I'm going to do."

"Well," Mrs. Smith said, "you know, of course, that I don't approve of any of this. I don't see why you can't stay quietly at home and play Halloween games."

Agnes buttoned her pajama jacket. It was too big and the sleeves were too long. Mrs. Smith, looking at her shining, light-brown hair, her delicate features, and her slender hands, smiled to herself. "She wouldn't frighten a mouse," she thought. Out loud, she said, "Mrs. Wagner says to be careful of her hammock. She'll send Harry down to get it from the pile at the end of the street in the morning. She asked me to tell you *please* to put it on the top of the pile, where it won't get torn."

"Oh, we'll do that, all right," Agnes said. "It's the Johnsons and the Waughops we're really after. They're the ones who'll wish they'd never been born."

"They will just about faint," Tootie said.

Mrs. Smith walked to the door and called across the hall, "You can make them up now, Father!"

Grandpa Prophater crossed the hall carrying two false faces, a piece of burnt cork, two small paper bags filled with flour, and two pieces of soap. He wore a maroon velvet smoking jacket and across his breast he had pinned a sheet of paper covered with strange hieroglyphics. Tootie and Agnes saw that he was also wearing his rubbers. He came into the room, placed the things he was carrying on the bed, and tapped at the paper on his chest. "Can't be too careful on a night like this," he said.

Tootie danced in front of him, the legs of her pajamas flapping. "What's it for?" she asked. "What does it *mean*?"

"What does it *mean*?" Grandpa Prophater repeated. "*That* I can't tell you. *That* is a secret I have with *him*." He pointed down to the floor.

"Papa?" Tootie asked.

"Papa!" Agnes exclaimed derisively. "He means the devil, of course. Don't you, Grandpa?"

Grandpa Prophater drew his thick eyebrows together in a frown and his black eyes sparkled. "Don't say that name," he whispered. "He doesn't like *anyone* to say his name."

"Now, Father," Mrs. Smith said.

"You're right, Anna," he said. He looked down at the sign and muttered to himself, as though he could read the strange words printed there.

"What have you got your rubbers on for?" Agnes asked.

"Protection," Grandpa Prophater answered. "There's been a little lightning in the air, even though the stars are out. If I were you, I'd wear my rubbers."

Tootie looked thoughtfully down at her feet. "I will," she said. She picked up her false face from the bed and fastened it on. It was a brightly colored face with a shock of red hair, a large, bulbous nose, and thick red lips. The holes for the nostrils came to the top of her upper lip and she had difficulty breathing. She held out her hands to Grandpa Prophater and he rubbed the backs of them with burnt cork.

Agnes' false face was a ghastly white skeleton's head. Below it, her slim white neck looked pink, and her braids shone in the soft gaslight.

Tootie screamed at the sight of her. "You look horrible! Simply horrible! I'd never know you!"

Agnes ran to the cheval glass and gasped. "I look terrible," she said. "I can't believe it's me." She turned toward Tootie. "You look terrible, too. You look like a drunken ghost."

"That's what I want to look like!" Tootie cried. "A drunken ghost! You're a horrible ghost and I'm a terrible drunken ghost."

"You were killed in a den of thieves," Agnes said. "And I died of a broken heart. I've never even been buried, simply because I was never found."

There was a rustling sound on the ground under the two front windows, followed by a loud groan. Grandpa Prophater clutched the sign on his chest and bowed his head. "You wouldn't catch me going out tonight," he said. "Not in a million years."

Agnes laughed, but there was no mirth in her laughter. "It's the girls," she said. "I'm pretty sure I heard Esther giggle."

"I dare you to go and see," Tootie said. "I dare you to go down the back stairs all alone."

Even in the daylight, Tootie never used the back stairs. At the landing, there was a purple-and-green stained-glass window, which admitted a subdued, ghostly light. Agnes ran to the doorway and looked across the hall. The hall light was on and the back stairs were not entirely dark. No weird light shone through the window at the landing. She hurried across the hall and down the stairs, while Tootie followed her, screaming. They ran through the kitchen into the dining room, where their father sat playing solitaire, and into the parlor, where Rose and Esther stood looking out of the big bay window.

"Have you been there all the time?" Agnes asked.

Rose turned around slowly, patting her

hair, which was twisted into a neat figure eight at the nape of her neck. "Oh, hello," she said. "Been where?"

"Where you are now," Agnes answered.

"Why, no, we haven't," Rose said. "We were reading, and we thought we heard a noise."

"Not that it could be anything, *really*," Esther said. "I mean even if it is Halloween, no one believes in ghosts any more."

"There's a leaf on your skirt," Agnes said.

Esther stooped and picked it off, crushing it in her fingers. "I was sweeping the path before dinner," she said.

Mr. Smith got up from the table and stood at the double doors that opened into the parlor. "What's this about ghosts?" he asked.

"Agnes and Tootie thought they heard one," Rose answered. "I told them no one who had any sense believed in ghosts."

"A ghost should hold no terrors for *you* after your staying up until twelve last night listening to the gibberings of that Wade fellow," Mr. Smith said. He looked at Agnes and Tootie. "Who are these two young boys?"

Agnes and Tootie screamed delightedly,

and Agnes ran toward her father and shook his arm. "It's me, Papa!" she cried. "Don't you know me? It's me. Agnes."

He lifted her false face. "So it is," he said. "Well, I must admit you had me fooled."

"We fooled him!" Tootie exclaimed proudly. "I guess if we fooled him, we can fool anybody."

Mrs. Smith came down the front stairs, followed by Grandpa Prophater, who was carrying the bags of flour and the two pieces of soap. "I think you'd better get started," Mrs. Smith said. "I don't want you out too late. Lonnie, tell them not to stay out too late."

Mr. Smith took out his watch and glanced at it. "Mind your mother," he said.

"You heard what your father said," Mrs. Smith told them. She went to the coat closet in the back hall and came back with Agnes' and Tootie's coats, which they slipped on obediently. Below Agnes' dark-blue coat and Tootie's brown one, their pajama pants and part of their pajama jackets showed. Grandpa Prophater handed them each a bag of flour and a piece of soap.

"When you ring the doorbells and people

answer, don't throw too much flour," Mrs. Smith said. "A small handful will be plenty. And when you come back, you can have some cider and doughnuts."

"Yes, Ma'am," Tootie said.

Mrs. Smith kissed her lightly on the top of her head and patted Agnes' shoulder. "Get along then," she said.

The night was sharp and clear, and the air smelled of damp leaves and apples. The two little girls stood for a moment on the porch after the door had closed behind them. "I don't see anybody," Tootie said.

Agnes looked up and down the street. "I don't either," she said. She breathed the night air in as deeply as she could through her mask, and the smell of it mingled strangely with the musty odor of the painted canvas.

"We might as well begin on the Wagners," Tootie said.

They walked sedately down the cement steps to the sidewalk, and along the sidewalk under the street lamp to the next house. Mrs. Wagner had taken her hammock from the hooks of her front porch and had laid it invit-

ST. LOUIS *October 1903*

ingly folded on the floor. The two little girls tiptoed up the steps and picked it up cautiously. Mrs. Wagner, hearing them, peeked through the curtains of the living room. "It's Tootie and Agnes," she whispered to her husband. "I'm glad they got here first. I told Anna to ask them to be careful, and I'm sure they will be. That is, I'm sure they *will* be careful unless Tootie gets carried away. She can be very rough when she gets carried away."

Agnes and Tootie walked silently down the street until suddenly, at the corner, they saw a flare of light. "There they are!" Tootie cried. "There are the rest of the kids. They're burning something."

"I don't think we'd better let them burn the hammock," Agnes said. "I don't think Mrs. Wagner would like it." She turned her false face toward Tootie, and through the sockets of the skeleton Tootie could see Agnes' eyes, gray and determined.

They carried Mrs. Wagner's hammock to the nearest lawn and put it down gently. Then they ran silently and swiftly toward the small, dark figures that danced around the sheet of flame at the end of the block. Although Agnes was six years older than Tootie, she could not run as fast. When Tootie ran it was as though nothing mattered except that she was going as fast as she could in the direction she wanted to go, while Agnes thought of how she looked running. Even in the dark she set her feet down daintily and swung her arms gracefully, conscious of her braids, hoping they weren't getting too mussed, reaching up occasionally to feel if her mask was at the proper angle. By the time she reached the group of children, Tootie was already throwing sticks and dried branches onto the fire. "I'm going to take the Johnsons," she was chanting.

"I'm going to take the Wades!" a boy shouted.

"The Weyricks! The Laceys! The Ferrises! The Tevises!" The shrill young voices called out the names of their victims.

Agnes stood back from the bonfire, panting a little. The dancing, screaming children frightened her more than the moans of the banshees down by the ashpit. As one of the children pushed her aside, she drew farther back into the shadows. Her hands were cold and the burnt cork made them feel dry. Tootie, dancing by, saw her standing there. "Look at Agnes!" she called. "Isn't she horrible! Isn't she the best! She looks the most terrible, so she should have the most terrible! She can have the Waughops!"

"The Waughops!" the children yelled. "Agnes Smith can have the Waughops!"

"The Waughops have a bulldog!" Tootie screeched. "Agnes may be torn to pieces by the Waughops' bulldog."

"I'm not afraid!" Agnes cried. She drew nearer the bonfire slowly and felt Tootie's warm hand in her own.

"You don't have to take the Waughops," Tootie said.

Agnes began to laugh. She reached down and picked up someone's doormat and threw it on the flames. "The Waughops for me!" she screamed. She swung Tootie violently around and ran up the street, passing the Laceys' house, the Ferrises', the Yules', the Weyricks', the Cavanaughs', the Wagners', her own house, and on until she reached the Waughops', which was the last house on the block. She stopped abruptly halfway up the slope of their terraced lawn. The soles of her feet tingled, her eyes smarted with tears, and her nose was running. She lifted her mask and wiped her nose on the edge of her pajama sleeve. There was a light in the Waughops' parlor, and through the curtains she could see Mr. and Mrs. Waughop. His head was bent over the evening paper, but the curve of his nose, the thick back of his neck, looked cruel and forbidding. Agnes remembered that the Waughops never hung a Christmas wreath on their door and that they never had a tree. She remembered the way Mrs. Waughop had looked at her the time she had almost bumped into her on her skates. She thought of the Waughops' bulldog and of how he slobbered and his eyes, which had a film over them.

Silently, she crept up the terrace. The ground was hard and slippery. The bench that usually stood at the edge of the lawn was not there and, glancing toward the porch, she saw that the chairs had been put away. She crept closer to the house until she stood beneath the parlor window, where she crouched, feeling the bricks with her cold, thin hand. The bricks felt hard and rough, and she noticed that they were a dirty shade of yellow and not warm and red like the bricks of her own house. It occurred to her that she was able to get so close to the house because there were no flowers or bushes planted there, not even the dried stumps of any. She listened, and could hear no leaves blowing across the lawn. She raised herself up cautiously until she could see plainly into the room. A round table stood in the center of the room and in the middle of the table was a lamp with a dark-green shade. There were no books or magazines littering the top of the table and the light from the lamp looked dim, and she wondered if it always burned as low. Mr. Waughop sat bent forward to the light and, as she watched, he turned a page without looking up. At a farther distance from the light, Mrs. Waughop sat, her hands folded in her lap, rocking.

Agnes watched them, fascinated. Her body grew cramped and her hands numb. Far down the block she could hear the children screaming, but she stayed silent, half stooping, looking through the window. She would not move, she thought, until one of them spoke. One by one, Mr. Waughop turned the pages of the paper until he reached the last. Then he folded the paper neatly and tucked it into the pocket of his coat. He looked at Mrs. Waughop, and Mrs. Waughop nodded. Without speaking, he reached to turn off the light.

Agnes stood up quickly and ran toward the porch, and as the light went off in the parlor she rang the bell. The bell sounded like a shriek to her, but she stood facing the door until a light was turned on in the hall and the door was opened. Mr. Waughop looked down at her, his bulldog slobbering and wheezing at his side, and in back of him, like a shadow, was Mrs. Waughop. Mr. Waughop didn't speak. And Agnes reached up with one hand and lifted her mask until it sat like a hat on the top of her head. Her gray eyes were clear but not childlike. She put her hand in her coat pocket, and drawing out a handful of flour, she threw it into his face. "I hate you, Mr. Waughop," she said, calmly. Then panic overtook her and she ran down the steps, across the lawns, sobbing, until she reached her own house. She hurried to the back of the house and through the back door into the kitchen.

Katie was stacking sugared doughnuts on

a large platter. She had changed into a clean apron that billowed out white and crisp against the soft blue of her dress. A tray with a pitcher of cider and over two dozen glasses were on the kitchen table. Katie looked up at Agnes, and the expression on her face, which had been placid, grew serious. "Agnes!" she said. "What have you been up to?"

Agnes threw her arms around Katie and buried her head in the white apron. "The Waughops!" she sobbed.

"What did they do to you, now?" Katie asked. "Say the word to me and I'll go down there myself."

"They didn't do anything," Agnes said. She drew away from Katie and looked at her solemnly. "I threw flour at him," she said. "I killed him."

Katie sat down in the rocking chair and drew Agnes toward her. "There, now," she said. "There, now." She began to talk quietly, and as she talked she slipped Agnes' coat from her shoulders and began to rip the soft material of the pajamas until they were almost in shreds.

"Now, dry your eyes," she said, "and

we'll go tell the folks. They're all in there, and more besides. Every no-account on the block."

She picked up the platter of doughnuts and, taking Agnes by the hand, she marched through the door into the dining room. The dining room was full of children. Tootie had got back and was sitting on her mother's lap, talking excitedly. Katie stooped to whisper in Agnes' ear, "Her and her lies." And then she lifted her head proudly and set the platter of doughnuts in the middle of the table. "Here's the one," she said, pulling Agnes forward. "Here's the one that's done it all. Here's the one that was chased to the back door of this very house with a fierce brute at her heels tearing her clothes to shreds." She picked a doughnut from the platter and stuffed it in Agnes' mouth. "The Waughops, the villains, are the people that this fearless child destroyed tonight."

Mrs. Smith moved Tootie gently from her lap and stood up. "Is she hurt?" she asked.

"Not a scratch on her," Katie said. "She outran that brute all the way from Waughops' to her own door in the pitch dark."

Grandpa Prophater pushed his way toward Agnes. He took a shred of her pajamas in his fingers and looked at it sharply. The pajamas, he noticed, were torn neatly in inch-wide strips from top to bottom, and they were very clean. He also noticed that Agnes wore no coat. He looked Katie straight in the eyes, and her eyes were blazing. "God help you, Katie Laughlin, when you enter your church Sunday morning," he said softly.

"I always told you," Katie said blandly, "that Agnes, for all she's so quiet, is the fiercest of the lot." Then she stepped back modestly so that the heroine could receive the acclaim that was due her from the common people.

November 1903

NOVEMBER 1903

Esther sat on the bed in the room she shared with her sister Rose and sighed deeply. In one hand she held a pair of manicure scissors and in the other a picture of Jan Kubelik which she had just cut out of the Sunday paper. "Shall we put him in the matinée-idol panel or the hero panel?" she asked.

Rose looked critically around the room. The bedroom set of bird's-eye maple shone brightly in the sunlight, the pale-blue bows that held back the soft, ruffled curtains were clean and carefully pressed, and the blue flowered wallpaper was fresh and new. Two strips of cheesecloth stretching from the molding to the floor had been tacked to the wall on either side of the head of the bed. And on these strips Esther and Rose had pasted pictures cut from magazines and newspapers—pictures of young men in football suits, pictures of actors—and photographs of dozens of boys. Rose's eyes traveled slowly down the hero panel, which hung to the left of the bed. "I don't think we should put him there," she said. "Not with DeWitt, even if DeWitt did make a drop kick that really won the game for Princeton."

"I don't think we'd better, either," Esther agreed. "It would be sort of a sacrilege. Especially if we put him near that horse."

Rose got up from the chair in front of the dressing table and walked over to the hero panel. On one side of the panel she had pasted a picture of a horse, a handsome creature who stood proudly while a man in a high silk hat held onto his reins with one hand and held a silver cup aloft with the other. "Of course, I'm utterly distracted over horses," she said. "But I suppose we really should put Kubelik in the matinée-idol panel."

"With the man who sang 'Under a Panama'?" Esther asked. "A man who sings in *minstrel* shows? Why, I've even forgotten his name."

"Delamotta is in the idol panel," Rose argued. "You didn't think anything about it when we put him in with a minstrel-show singer. He's a great artist, too. He's wonderful in love scenes *and* tragic parts. I didn't blame Carmen a bit for being crushed on him."

ST. LOUIS *November 1903*

"She didn't stay crushed on him very long," Esther said. "And I might add that the idol panel was good enough for Prince Henry of Prussia, who has never even been on the stage."

Rose turned away from the panel, her hands on her hips and her eyes staring across the top of Esther's head into space. The music of a violin was in her ears, and a lump was in her throat. "Look, Ess," she said. "He simply can't go in *either* panel. We've got to make another panel for him. A *genius* panel. Lots of people say that Kubelik is a second Paganini, but I *know* he is."

"I wouldn't say that," Esther said. "I must say that I wasn't *horribly* impressed with his playing of the first two movements. If you must know, I was more impressed by his *fascinating* eyes, the way they snapped and danced, and the way his wonderful hair shook during the strenuous parts."

"Well, I'm not a music critic," Rose said. "I don't set myself up to be one. But you must admit Mamma is, and she says that his slow movements are even lovelier than his other ones when he is in the mood for them."

"I know," Esther said. "But a *genius*. I

think you've got to be careful about simply coming out and saying someone's a genius."

Rose picked up the picture of Jan Kubelik and looked at it thoughtfully. He was young and his hair was very black. "If Kubelik isn't a genius, he certainly looks like one," she said. "And that's almost as satisfactory."

"Well, then, I'll get the cheesecloth." Esther got up from the bed and walked to the closet. There was a roll of cheesecloth on the lower shelf, and she took it out and handed it to Rose. "You'd better hang it. You're taller," she said.

Rose pulled the straight dressing-table chair to the wall opposite the foot of the bed. "I think we should have the genius panel facing us, so we can see it the last thing before we put out the light," she said. "It might do something for us."

"It might," Esther answered. "As a matter of fact, I think we talk too much about *boys*. I think we should really try to get our minds off them."

Rose held the strip of cloth along the edge of the molding. "Just hand me some pins," she said. "I think I can make it stay up with pins by sticking them through the cloth and under the wood. I don't think we'd better ask Mamma for the hammer." She fastened the panel to the wall, top and bottom, and then she stood back and looked at it. "Don't you think it's kind of plain?" she asked. "I mean for a genius panel?"

Esther squinted her eyes, tilted her head back, and looked at it through her lashes. "It *is* plain," she said. "He'll look funny there all by himself. Do you think we might put James K. Hackett with him? He was wonderful in 'The Crisis,' and he's one of the dearest things on earth."

Rose dropped her arms limply at her sides and pressed her lips together. "You don't get the point at all," she said. "James K. Hackett is not a genius. I merely meant that Kubelik ought to have some flowers around him, or a design, or something. You paste him on and I'll look for something. Paste him in the middle, because no matter what other geniuses we find, we'll always remember that Kubelik was the first genius we ever laid eyes on." She opened the top drawer of her bureau and searched through it hurriedly. She took out a piece of silver paper that had been in a candy box and a length of purple ribbon that had come wrapped around a bunch of violets. She fluted the paper into a fan shape and tied the ribbon into a bow at the end. Carefully, she pinned it on the cheesecloth under Kubelik's picture. "It isn't what I would like, exactly," she said. "But it will do for the time being."

"We should really have a wreath. A laurel wreath," Esther said.

"We really should," Rose said. They stood in front of the picture, their arms around each other's waists. Rose, glancing sideways into the dressing-table mirror, thought they made a picture. She leaned her head down until it rested against Esther's soft black hair. "It would have been nice," she said, "if I could have been a blonde. We practically could have done anything then. Imagine how we would have looked going out together, you with your dark hair and me with radiant blonde hair."

"It's nice we don't look alike, though," Esther said. "If we looked alike, we might think we had to dress alike, and that would be appalling! Think how I'd look in your white dress with the yellow sash."

They turned without thinking away from Kubelik, the genius, and faced the mirror. Rose fluffed out her pompadour with her fingers and Esther bit her lips to make them redder. Their faces were pretty, bland, and, for a moment, fatuous.

From somewhere outside the house there was a piercing shriek. Rose turned quickly away and started for the door. "It's Tootie," she said. "What's she bawling about?"

"Maybe Mamma said she'd give her a good whipping," Esther answered.

"Not on Sunday," Rose said. "I don't think Mamma would promise her a whipping on Sunday." She opened the door, and there was another shriek.

The two girls stood in the doorway. They could hear the kitchen door bang shut and someone running down the walk at the back of the house. They ran across the upstairs hall and into the bathroom, where, by opening the window and leaning out, they could see most of the walk. Their mother was running in the direction of the shrieks, which seemed to be coming from the alley, which was hidden by the woodshed and the brick ashpit. She wore the clothes she had worn to church, a gray broadcloth dress with a full skirt, which she held high as she ran, showing her white petticoat. She was sobbing and crying out, "Tootie! Where are you? Answer me, Tootie!"

Rose stepped back from the window and covered her eyes. "The trolley!" she screamed. "I heard it shake the house when we were in our room. I'm almost sure I heard it shake the house."

Esther turned toward her, and her face was white. "You mean she was walking the tracks and . . ."

They stared at one another. Then, fleet as deer, they ran through the hall and down the back stairs, across the kitchen, and down onto the path. Their mother had disappeared, and they ran along the path, passing the woodshed, which smelled of rats, through the back gate, into the alley. The alley was paved unevenly with bricks from the back-yard fences to the place where it sloped to the trolley tracks. They peered down the incline and along the tracks, which glittered in the cold sunlight, but even down as far as the curve, there was no sign of Tootie. "She's still screaming somewhere," Rose said. "I can hear her."

"Maybe Mamma carried her into Mrs. Wagner's," Esther said. She gave a fearful look at the tracks again to see if there was any sign of blood, and at that moment Mrs. Smith came out through the Wagners' back gate into the alley, carrying Tootie in her arms. From where they stood they could see that Tootie's face was bloody and that her dress was dirty and covered with cinders.

Rose and Esther walked toward their mother slowly. "What can we do, Mamma?" Rose asked. "What can we do?"

Their mother's head was bent over Tootie, and she walked blindly, stumbling a little on the bricks. Esther ran ahead and opened the gate. "Get your father," Mrs. Smith said. "Get your father. He's at the Joneses'."

Esther cut across the lawn toward the front of the house, and Rose followed her mother and Tootie miserably up the path. Tootie had stopped screaming. Her eyes were open, and the expression in them was not one of pain. Rose, watching, saw that Tootie's eyes were blazing. "Mamma," Rose began.

But her mother didn't hear her. The tears streamed down her face, and she seemed broken and pathetic. "Oh, Rose," she sobbed. "Get the doctor. If you can't get Dr. Bond, get Dr. Thierry."

Rose glanced sharply down at Tootie. "I'll telephone, Mamma," she said. "It will be quicker." They walked slowly up the steps, and Rose held the door open while Mrs. Smith carried Tootie through. As they passed into the living room, Tootie began to scream again. But this time it seemed to Rose that her screams were forced. Mrs. Smith laid her down on the sofa and, taking a handkerchief from her sleeve, gently wiped Tootie's face. "Don't try to talk," she said. "Mother's baby."

Tootie lay back on the cushions. Her screams had stopped again and she looked up at her mother. "He tried to kill me," she said. Her hands were clenched at her sides and her small body was tense.

"If I only knew where that blood was coming from!" Mrs. Smith said. "Rose, bring a basin and some water."

"He tried to kill me," Tootie repeated.

Mrs. Smith bent over her. "Hurry!" she called to Rose. "I think it's her lip!"

ST. LOUIS *November 1903*

Rose came back into the living room with a basin of water and a soft cloth. Tootie, seeing the basin, began to cry again. "Mother won't hurt her baby," Mrs. Smith said. She took the cloth and washed the blood from Tootie's face. There was a scratch on her forehead and one on her cheek, and her lip was cut through and swollen. Her mother gently lifted the lip and gave a small shriek. "She's chipped her tooth!" she cried.

The front door opened and closed, and Mrs. Smith turned and ran to her husband, burying her face in his shoulder.

"Now then, Anna," Mr. Smith said. "Now then. What's happened?"

"He tried to kill me," Tootie said.

"Don't try to tell us now," her father said. "Just lie quietly until the doctor comes."

"The doctor!" Mrs. Smith exclaimed. "Rose forgot all about him."

"I called him," Mr. Smith said, patting her shoulder. "I called him from the Joneses'." He leaned over Tootie and felt her thin little legs and her small, sharp elbows. "How did it happen?"

"It was the streetcar," Esther said. "It hit her. It must have tossed her right onto the cinders at the side of the track. Didn't it, Tootie?"

Tootie shook her head from side to side. "It wasn't the streetcar," she said. "It was Barton. He tried to kill me."

Mr. Smith straightened up and squared his shoulders. "Barton Wagner?" he asked. "Barton Wagner hit *you*?"

"He tried to kill me," Tootie said, her voice coming indistinctly from her swelling lips. "And when I screamed, he ran away. Agnes ran, too. But she ran *before*. She ran before he tried to kill me."

There was a ring at the door, and Mrs. Smith, murmuring thankfully, "The doctor," hurried to let him in. He came into the room, a tall, thin young man, and set his bag on the floor beside the couch. "Well, Tootie," he said cheerfully, "what is it this time?"

"Barton Wagner hit her, Dr. Thierry," Rose said. She looked at him approvingly. "And Barton's *much* older. He's as old as Esther."

Dr. Thierry bent down and examined the cut on Tootie's lip. "He hit her, all right," he said. "Or someone did. I'm afraid I'll have to take a couple of stitches here." He ran his hands expertly over her body. "No bones broken, though."

"A couple of stitches," Mr. Smith repeated. He caught his wife's hand. "We'll see about this. I think I'd like to have a talk with a young man who'd hit a little girl who isn't even half his age."

Mrs. Smith, Rose, and Esther watched him proudly as he left the room and slammed the front door behind him.

Dr. Thierry, bending over Tootie, said, "She's got something in her hand." He tried to loosen her fingers, but she clenched her fist tighter.

"Come, Tootie darling," Mrs. Smith said. "Give the doctor whatever it is you have in your hand."

Tootie's fist opened reluctantly and Dr. Thierry picked out a bloody mass and looked at it thoughtfully. "It's hair," he said. "Dark hair. I suppose, in fighting him off, she got a grip on his hair and pulled. She must have pulled very hard, because most of this hair has the roots on it. Well, I'm glad you hurt him some anyway, because that lip of yours is going to hurt you for a few days."

As he opened his bag, Rose and Esther turned aside and shuddered. Mrs. Smith took Tootie's small hand in her own and turned her face away. There was silence in the room for some time. Finally Dr. Thierry stood up, his voice cheerful. "Well, that's over," he said.

"Over!" Esther cried. "And she didn't even cry!"

"Of course she didn't cry," Mrs. Smith said. "Tootie never cries. She may have cried a little at first, but what child wouldn't?"

Tootie's lip was covered with a small bandage, and two streaks of iodine covered the scratches on her face. She smiled up at her mother.

"Why, she can even smile," Mrs. Smith said. "I don't know when I've seen such a brave little girl. Now, Dr. Thierry, do you think bed?" She pointed significantly at the ceiling.

"I think she'd better be put to bed," he answered. "She's had a lot of excitement for one day." He wrote hurriedly on a prescription blank. "And I'll leave this at the drugstore on my way home and one of the girls can get it later." He pushed Tootie's hair back from her face. "You're a good little girl, Tootie," he said.

Rose and Esther followed him to the door. "Thank you a million times," Rose said. She smiled at him sweetly. "I guess no one realizes how much *good* a doctor does until one is confronted with an emergency." She swayed toward Esther and they automatically put their heads together in the pose they had taken in front of the mirror. Their bright eyes were admiring, and Dr. Thierry thought how fresh and unspoiled they were for such very pretty girls. It was what they wanted him to think.

"Goodbye," they said.

"Goodbye," he answered. He turned away so quickly that the pocket of his coat caught on the doorknob. Rose loosed it gently, and Esther laughed so that her dimples would show. They watched him as he ran down the steps and turned to the left, which was the wrong direction to take to get to the drugstore.

"Esther!" Mrs. Smith said sharply. "I wish you'd stop standing there grinning like an ass at a thistle and help me get the baby to bed."

"I'll carry her," Rose said. She took Tootie

from her mother's arms and started up the stairs.

"I want to go to bed in your room," Tootie said.

"In my room!" Rose repeated. "What makes you want to go to bed in my room?"

"It's so pretty," Tootie said.

"Mamma, can Tootie go to bed in our room?" Rose asked.

"She can go to bed in any room she wants," Mrs. Smith said.

Tootie buried her head in Rose's neck and sighed. "I like to be carried," she said. "It's like floating."

At the top of the stairs Esther ran ahead and turned down the covers of the bed. Mrs. Smith hurried to the bathroom and ran the hot water. "We'll wash her little face and hands," she said.

Esther opened the drawer of her dresser and brought out a white nightgown trimmed with lace and embroidered at the yoke. "And she can wear this," she said. "Wear it until she gets ready to go to sleep, anyway. Let's dress her up."

"Let's," Rose said. "Remember what fun we had dressing her up when she was a baby?"

ST. LOUIS   *November 1903*

They took off Tootie's shoes and stockings and carefully slipped her clothes over her head. It was simple to get her into the nightgown, which was too big for her, and by the time Mr. Smith came in Tootie was sitting up in bed, a pink ribbon around her hair, sipping lemonade through a straw. When her father came into the room she glanced at him out of the corners of her eyes and sipped slowly.

"Well," Mrs. Smith asked, "what did he have to say for himself."

Mr. Smith stooped and kissed Tootie on her shining curls. "There wasn't much for him to say. Wagner, I mean. I didn't see Barton. I just told Wagner the whole story, and he apologized. I told him an apology wasn't enough, so he's going to have a talk with the boy."

"A talk!" Esther cried. "Isn't he even going to punish him?"

"He tried to kill me," Tootie said. "I hit him back."

"Wagner couldn't find him," Mr. Smith said. "You don't have to worry. Wagner will punish him when he comes home tonight."

"He's hiding!" Esther said. "The horrible little coward!"

"He'll be back," Mr. Smith said calmly. He took a cigar from his pocket and bit the end off it. "Now, Anna, how about a little supper?"

Mrs. Smith got up from the bed, where she had been sitting stroking Tootie's feet under the covers. "I suppose we must eat. You two girls stay here with Tootie, in case she wants anything."

Esther stood in the middle of the room, her eyes black and shining. She waited until she heard her mother's and father's footsteps in the kitchen below before she spoke. "I'm going to tell Grandpa when he comes home," she said. "He'll do something. He was a soldier. Papa didn't do anything. Why, Mr. Wagner even gave him a cigar."

"What can Grandpa do?" Rose asked. "He can only talk to him the way Papa did."

Esther walked to the dressing table and took the bow from her hair. She took off her shirtwaist and, going to the closet, pulled a middy blouse from a hook and slipped it over her head. "Now!" she said.

"What are you going to do?" Rose asked.

ST. LOUIS *November 1903*

"What am I going to do? I'm going to find that sneaking Barton Wagner and beat the jelly out of him."

"Esther!" Rose cried. "It isn't *ladylike* to fight. Besides, I think he kind of likes you."

"Nevertheless," Esther said, "I'm going to beat him up."

Tootie blew into the straw, making bubbles at the bottom of the glass. "Again?" she said.

Esther hurried from the room and ran down the stairs. Rose sighed, and moved over to the window. It was dark out and misty. The street light in front of the Wagners' house was blurred. She shuddered when she thought of Esther battling Barton Wagner in the dark, and she frowned, vaguely disapproving of the whole thing.

"Poor Barton," Tootie said. "He shouldn't have tried to kill me."

She drew designs on the blanket with a finger and crunched small bits of ice with her back teeth.

It seemed a long time to Rose before the front door opened and Esther ran up the stairs. Her hair was mussed and her hands were dirty.

Her middy blouse was torn at the collar. She dusted her hands together. "I got him," she said.

Rose put her arms around Esther and hugged her. "Where did you find him?" she asked. "What did he have to say for himself?"

"Say for himself!" Esther's laugh was coarse. "He didn't have a chance to say anything for himself. I simply stood before him and drew myself up and said, 'Barton Wagner, I've come to teach you not to hit a six-year-old girl.' And then I let him have it. He was in his own back yard, too. He never even got a chance to scratch me."

"Your middy blouse is torn," Rose said.

"It got torn while he was trying to hold me off," Esther said. "When I got close enough, I bit him."

"I bit him, too," Tootie said. "But he scratched me when he was trying to hold me off. Agnes said we'd better run for our lives, but I was too mad. He dragged us all the way from the corner and tried to hide us in his woodshed."

"He tried to *hide* you?" Rose asked. She walked over to the bed and looked Tootie squarely in the eye. "Why was he trying to *hide* you?"

There was a slight sound at the door and Agnes came into the room. She wore her coat, her stocking cap was pushed back on her head, and her eyes were shining with excitement. "I saw the whole thing, Tootie," she said. "You should have run when I did, and you would have seen the whole thing, too."

Tootie sat up in bed and bent forward eagerly. "What happened?" she asked.

Agnes pulled off her cap and threw it on the bed. "How'd you get scratched?"

"Barton," Tootie answered.

"Oh," Agnes said. "Well, when I got loose from him I ran back, and there was a big crowd. There was a policeman, and he was pretty mad, let me tell you. So was everyone in the trolley mad."

"Did it go off the track?" Tootie asked.

"No, it didn't go off the track, exactly," Agnes said. "But the cable came off. They had quite a time getting it back on. It came off when the motorman put on the brakes so fast."

"I was there when he put on his brakes.

I was there when the sparks began to fly out. But I would have liked to have seen the people so mad," Tootie said.

"It didn't hurt the dress at all," Agnes said. "I got it back in the excitement. Well, I didn't get it back, exactly. I *asked* for it. I asked the policeman. He said sure I could have it. I said I wanted it to dress up in."

"Listen," Esther said firmly, sitting down on the bed. "What is this that happened?"

"Nothing really happened," Agnes said. "The streetcar didn't go off the track. We thought it would, but it didn't."

"The thing we made looked just like a body," Tootie said. "A live body, too."

"It was that old dress Mamma gave us," Agnes explained, a little impatiently. "We had a wonderful idea, and we stuffed it and put it on the tracks. We thought when the motorman put on the brakes the streetcar would go right off the tracks."

"Agnes Smith," Rose said, "you're nothing more or less than a murderer. You might have killed dozens of people."

Agnes threw herself back on the bed wearily. "Oh, Rose," she said, "you're so stuck-up.

We were on the streetcar once when it went off the tracks and nobody got hurt. It just bumped us a little."

"The time we got our new shoes," Tootie said. "It only bumped us a little."

"Listen to me, Tootie," Esther said quietly. "How did you get that lip?"

Agnes and Tootie exchanged patient glances. Tootie's voice, when she spoke, was kind, as though she were talking to a baby. "Agnes and I put the lady on the track, and when Barton saw the streetcar coming and heard the bump, he dragged us up the alley and tried to make us stay in the woodshed. I was trying to get away, and he was trying to kill me. He wanted to hide us in the woodshed so the policeman wouldn't get us." She laughed amusedly. "As though policemen ever pay any attention to *girls!*"

"As though they did," Agnes echoed. "Tootie and I thought that if they arrested anybody they would arrest some of those boys."

"So I had to hit Barton," Tootie went on, "until he heard Mamma coming and ran."

Esther grabbed Tootie and shook her. "Get

out of this bed," she said. "And take that nightgown off."

"Oh, Ess," Rose said gently. "Leave her alone. After all, she was good about her lip and didn't cry."

"I *didn't* cry," Tootie said. "I didn't cry even when I fell down and hit my tooth. Did I, Agnes?"

"No, she didn't," Agnes answered loyally. "We were running up the bank after we put the body on the tracks and Tootie had a terrible fall. She didn't cry a speck."

Esther's hand came up in the air slowly, and then dropped again. She turned to Rose, and they both stared at their little sisters. Suddenly they began to laugh. They clung to one another and laughed until the tears streamed down their faces. "Ess," Rose cried, "we ought to take down Jan Kubelik's picture and put up Tootie's and Agnes's. We don't need any Bohemian violinist here when we've got a couple of geniuses in our own house."

Agnes and Tootie looked at them mildly. Then Tootie reached over and plucked at Agnes's sleeve. "How mad were they?" she asked. "All those people?"

December 1903

DECEMBER 1903

It was the week before Christmas, and Tootie sat on the floor of the upstairs hall directly under the telephone. She was writing on a pad of paper that she held in her lap. She held the pencil so tight that the thumb and forefinger of her right hand were bent backward, and as she wrote she thrust her tongue out in a sharp red point. "Dear Santy Claus, I want a tin kitching and a slad and some dolls jewlry. If you bring a tree put it in Lons room. Granpa says there is no room for trees this year so put it in Lons room. I want a red slad with pictures on it. I want a picture of raindeers on it. I hope the brownies will take this to you. I have been good. With love from Tootie Smith."

She tore the letter she had written away from the rest of the pad, folded it into a square, and then got up and knocked on the door of her grandfather's room. "Grandpa," she asked, "can I use your window this time?"

Her grandfather opened his door and stood

looking down at her. He saw that her expression was anxious and unusually mild. "Come in," he said gruffly, stepping aside to let her pass. The air in the small room was heavy with cigar smoke, and the bed was mussed where he had been lying on it. On the floor was a black-and-red striped Navajo rug, and on one wall was a large steel engraving of the Battle of Gettysburg. Under the engraving was Grandpa Prophater's sword in its scabbard. There were rust stains at the hilt; Tootie had always thought they were blood.

"There's not much use in putting that note on the window sill," Grandpa Prophater said. "There was a brownie around a few minutes ago, and he was pretty mad. He told me that he'd heard somebody snarling around here this morning."

Tootie eyed him sharply. "Which brownie was it?" she asked.

"The Dude." Grandpa Prophater shook his head and frowned. "And you know how he is. He can't stand snarling. He's the most delicate of all the brownies, and he has a weak stomach from eating too much candy and too many sour pickles."

"I didn't hear anybody snarling," Tootie said. "Unless Agnes might have been. She snarls a lot." She walked over to the window and put her note outside on the window sill.

Grandpa Prophater puffed on his cigar and then said, "I'm not going to hang up a sock this year."

Tootie turned away from the window and gasped. "You're not!"

"Nope," he said. "And I'll tell you why, if you won't tell any of the girls."

"I won't," Tootie promised. "I wouldn't for anything in this world."

"Well," Grandpa Prophater said, "a sock is too small. It's smaller than your stocking. It doesn't hold enough. So what I'm going to do is hang up my union suit."

Tootie looked horrified. "But you did that last year!" she said. "You tried the same thing. And look what happened. Santy Claus filled your union suit with coal and rotten potatoes. He did it because you were too greedy."

"Well, he won't do it this time," Grandpa Prophater said. "I got a little tip from the Dude that he won't do it this time. Because this year I'm going to hang it from the chandelier, so that it'll be the first thing Santa sees when he comes down the chimney. By the time he's filled it there won't be anything left for the stockings."

Tootie glanced at the note on the window sill. It was growing dark outside. "I asked for a tree," she said.

Grandpa Prophater snorted. "A tree!" he said. "There won't be any tree, let me tell you! Why, your mother's got the parlor so full of furniture that you couldn't *squeeze* a tree into it."

"Santy could put the tree in Lon's room," Tootie said.

"He *could*," Grandpa Prophater admitted, "but he won't." He walked toward the window and looked out. "I don't see a sign of the Dude. And your note's still there. Might as well bring it in before it blows away."

"I'll put a marble on it, and then it won't blow," Tootie said. She fished in her apron pocket and brought out a marble. "It's a chipped one." She lifted the window and set the marble on the slip of paper.

"I have a strange feeling that there isn't going to be any Christmas this year," Grandpa

ST. LOUIS *December 1903*

Prophater said. He shrugged his shoulders. "Oh, maybe a few oranges and figs and dates that your mother will buy. But nothing else." He spoke with forced cheerfulness. "Of course, we can buy a tree and trim it ourselves. Trim it with nice red berries, and walnuts and nigger-toes, or whatever we can scrape up."

Tootie's eyes filled with tears. "I don't want an orphan's tree," she said.

"It'll be better than nothing," he said. He watched her as she moved slowly toward the door.

"I don't know why Santy's so mad," she said. "Nobody's done anything bad around here. Nobody's beaten any horses, like Snarr's grocery boy does. Nobody's done any swearing, and nobody's lost anything." She opened the door and went out, shutting it softly.

Grandpa Prophater opened the window, put the marble in the pocket of his velvet smoking jacket, and read the note before he slipped it into the top drawer of his desk. "Tootie!" he called.

She ran back into his room. "What happened?" she asked. "Something terrible?"

"No," he said. "It looks pretty good. It

doesn't look as black as it did. The note's gone. The Dude probably came and took it while we were talking."

"Oh!" she cried, and ran screaming across the hall. In Rose's and Esther's room, her mother stood looking out of the window. "Be quiet, Tootie," she said automatically. "I won't be able to hear the hack if you make so much noise."

"Are they taking a *hack?*" Tootie asked. Her brother Lon was due to arrive from Princeton. His train was already three hours late. Tootie stared at her two sisters. Rose stood before the dressing table in a corset, ruffled drawers, and a hand-embroidered corset cover.

Esther stood off and nodded her head approvingly. "Mamma was right," she said. "You were ruining your figure."

"Well, I can't say I relish the idea of wearing one," Rose said. "But for tonight I'll do *anything*. Pride has simply come to my rescue, even if this corset is too long on the hips." She sat down on the chair in front of the dressing table. "It pokes my legs," she said. "And the steel affects my ribs unpleasantly. I don't see how I'm going to stoop. And the garters hurt."

"You look grand!" Esther said. "Simply elegant."

"I wonder what Lucille Pintard will be like," Rose said. "Probably one of those snobs."

"I can't imagine Lon getting crushed on a snob," Esther said. "I wonder if he has changed, and if he will look Eastern. I hope he has an Eastern-looking collar, like Roy Dunham's."

Mrs. Smith pushed aside the curtains and looked down the street. "I'm just anxious to see him," she said. "And I don't care whether he has a derby hat or a new-style collar or not."

"I don't, either," Tootie said. She walked over to her mother and pushed against her, like a pony. Her mother wore a satin shirtwaist and smelled of the Jicky perfume that she put on for special occasions.

"Well, naturally, Ess and I are keen to see him," Rose said. "But then I think it will be awfully exciting having a Princeton man pop in and stay a while."

"He'll have a derby hat, all right," Esther said. "I don't suppose Lucille Pintard would have given him a look if he hadn't."

"I don't see why you're acting so silly about a girl you've never even seen," Mrs. Smith said. "She's probably a very sweet young girl."

Esther's eyes flashed. "We happen to know she's *not*," she said. "We happen to know that when Lon took her to a dance in the East she ignored him all evening and danced with Harry Jewett the whole time. Roy Dunham was there and he told Abbie Gilroy. Abbie says this girl thinks she's a *queen*. And we know she's just coming to St. Louis to snub the whole town, *except* Harry Jewett. And even Helen Stuyvesant says she wouldn't have asked her to visit except that the invitation was practically wrung out of her."

"I don't think the invitation was *wrung* out of Helen at all, if you ask me," Rose said. "Helen's as homely as a mud fence, and she just wanted to make sure of getting to all the parties herself. And the best way to do that is to have a perfect queen staying with you."

"I hear something coming down the street!" Mrs. Smith cried. "It's probably your father and Lon." She turned from the window, her face flushed with excitement. For a minute she stood facing them all, and then, picking up her

ST. LOUIS *December 1903*

skirts, she ran across the room, out into the hall, and down the stairs. Rose reached for her kimono, her hands shaking, and Esther fastened it around her. They hugged one another and hurried from the room.

Tootie began to cry. She cried softly at first, and then worked herself up to piercing shrieks. When the shrieks had reached their height, she turned and stumbled down the stairs. The front door was open, and the air from the outside smelled of snow. At the threshold of the door, Lon had been stopped by his mother, who clung to him, and behind her Esther and Rose stood waiting their turn. He had a mandolin case in one hand and his hat in the other. Agnes tugged at the back of his coat. She was blue with the cold. "Lon! Lon!" she cried. "I've been sitting on the cement steps since your train was *due*! I didn't move once! I saw the hack before anybody. A tramp came by, and I didn't even move!"

Lon's face and neck were red with pleasure and embarrassment. His light-chestnut hair fell forward to the tops of his eyebrows as he bent to kiss his sisters. "You're too thin," his mother said. "I knew you'd be too thin." She glanced over his shoulder and saw her husband coming up the steps, carrying Lon's two bags.

"Lonnie," she said, "didn't you notice he was too thin?"

"Wait until you see your room," Esther said. "It looks grand, and the whole house looks Christmasy. I don't know how many packages have come so far."

"For the love of Pete," Lon said, "what's the matter with Tootie?" Tootie stood at the bottom of the stairs, still screaming. Hearing her name, she rushed toward Lon and threw herself in his arms. "Don't do it!" she cried. "Don't do it! It will bust up the whole thing. We don't need anybody else in this house. We haven't room! You can tell her we just haven't the room. You can tell her that we're perfectly all right as we are. Tell her that we don't need any extra help or anything."

Lon set his mandolin case on the floor and his derby hat on the piano stool. Then he stooped and picked Tootie up in his arms. "Tell who?" he asked. "What are you talking about, Tootie?"

"Tell that Lucille Pintard," Tootie said. "You can be polite if you want to."

"Look, Tootie," he said. "She isn't going to stay here."

Tootie stiffened and her eyes grew hard. "Why did she come to St. Louis then?" she asked. "Why does she think she's such a queen? I wouldn't marry a girl who thought she was such a queen. I wouldn't marry a girl named *Lucille!*"

"Look here," Lon said. "Who's getting married? Not me. Now quiet down. Did you ever hear of anyone getting married when he was still in college?" He set her gently down on the floor and spanked her twice, sharply.

He turned his back to them and lifted the mandolin case to the top of the piano. When he faced them again, he was composed and his lips were set. "I think I'll run up and say hello to Grandpa."

"And I'll hurry Katie up with dinner," Mrs. Smith said. "If you're all going out."

Mr. Smith and Lon picked up the suitcases and went up the stairs. Esther and Rose waited until they had gone. "Listen," Esther said to Tootie, "I've a notion to shake you until your teeth rattle. You're just a runny-nose little brat."

"I think," Tootie said, "I'll see if the table's set for dinner. I think I'll see if Katie has everything on. If everybody helped with the work in this house, we'd be all right." Without looking at her sisters, she walked through the back door that led to the kitchen.

"Tootie goes too far," Agnes said. "She's all right until she goes too far."

Rose turned on her. "You keep out of this, too!" she said. "We have enough trouble on our hands now." She put her arm in Esther's and they walked softly up the stairs. The door to Grandpa Prophater's room was closed, and through it came the sound of male voices, a low, comfortable murmur.

"You see," Rose said. "We're shut out. I don't see how men can just go places and close doors. I think it's the meanest thing they do. Grandpa does it most of the time, and even Papa does it sometimes, and now Lon's doing it. We've just got to think of something or we won't have any fun at all during the holidays."

"We can shut *our* door, too," Esther said. "There's nothing to prevent us."

In their room, Rose undid her garters and

breathed a sigh of relief. "I feel like an ossified woman in a sideshow," she said. She sat down on the bed.

"Tonight will be awful now that Lon knows we know about Lucille," Esther said.

"Awful," Rose agreed. "It was all right planning to snub her, but we can't even do that now. It will just get Lon down on both of us."

"I suppose it will." Esther sat at the dressing table and began to take the hairpins from her head. Her soft black hair fell below her shoulders, straight and fine.

Rose watched her for a minute, and then she sat up abruptly. "Ess," she said, "with your hair down that way you look just like a gypsy. You know, not like a real gypsy but like a stage one."

"I don't feel like a gypsy," Esther said.

Rose got up from the bed and, reaching for the hairbrush, began to brush Esther's hair violently. "I have an idea," she said. "We'll go as types."

"You mean—"

"Exactly," Rose said. "There are only twenty men worth paying any attention to who'll be there tonight, and we can handle twenty men, I should hope."

"I don't think I can handle twenty," Esther said. "I really don't."

"Look," Rose said. "I didn't say you had to handle the whole twenty. I just want you to guarantee eight or ten of them. I'll take the rest. I've already got about—let's see." She closed her eyes. "I've already got six, practically in the palm of my hand."

"And I've got about three or four," Esther said. "I've got Ralph, Sam, Warren, and George."

"And we'll both make a beeline for Harry Jewett. It'll be perfect," Rose said. "Because they're not going to fill in the dance cards until people get there, and if we get there early, looking like *types*, we shouldn't have any trouble at all. I think I'll be the queenly type."

"Lucille Pintard is the queenly type. Abbie said so. I don't think you could be as queenly as a girl from the East who's had lots of practice."

"I can be queenly," Rose said. "I can wear my dress with the yellow sash just as I planned, but I don't have to wear my corsage at my waistline. I can wear some of the yellow roses in my hair, and I can carry Mamma's black lace fan."

"It's December," Esther said. "What would you do with a fan?"

Rose laughed lightly. "I'll use it to flirt with. I'll use it to look different. And you, Ess, you can be a sort of minx. I'll cut your hair even with your shoulders and you can wear it *down*."

"I won't wear it down," Esther protested. "I'll look too young."

"You're not going to act young," Rose told her. "You're going to act vibrant. I'll take the men who like my type and you take the ones who like to romp around. And don't forget your dimples."

"I'll wear a red sash," Esther said, "and I'll swish my skirts a lot."

They smiled at each other. Rose took a pair of scissors from the bureau drawer. "I guess," she said, "Miss Lucille Pintard will be glad to dance with Lon when she sees what's left."

At one o'clock that night, Mrs. Smith came

down from the third floor, where she had been unpacking Lon's things, and went into her own room. Her husband lay in bed reading. Looking at the worn cover, Mrs. Smith knew instantly that the book was "Pickwick Papers."
"You'll ruin your eyes," she said.

Mr. Smith glanced up. His eyes were clear and brown, and he wore no glasses. He had been reading in bed all his life—by a kerosene lamp turned low when he was a boy in Wisconsin, by a dim overhead gaslight in boarding-houses when he was a young man, and now, in the high-backed black-walnut bed, by an electric chandelier that hung from the ceiling. He put down his book and yawned. Mrs. Smith walked over and sat down in the small rocking chair by the window.

"I should have waited and put the clean curtains up just before Christmas," she said. "They're dirty already."

"They look fine," he said. He sat up and looked out into the dark night. "It's started to snow."

His wife leaned forward and parted the curtains. "So it has," she said. "And the girls didn't take their overshoes. Well, they'll be home soon, and there are only a few flakes coming down. I hope Lon won't stay too late saying goodbye to that Lucille Pintard. Did you take the notes Tootie left on the window sills?"

"Yes," he answered. "But I couldn't find one of the letters that Agnes hid. She told me she wrote six, but I could only find five. She hides them in the chimneys as a rule."

"I'm not sure that Agnes quite believes in the brownies," Mrs. Smith said. "It's too bad. She's probably hidden that note somewhere to test them. I'll ask Papa if he found it." She got up from the chair and went to the door and called softly across the hall.

Grandpa Prophater came out of his room. His hair was mussed. In his hands he carried two small white figures which he had made out of handkerchiefs. The figures had queer, twisted arms and legs, thin bodies, and round white heads. Black threads were attached to the heads, arms, and legs, so he could make them dance like marionettes.

"Did you find a letter that Agnes hid?" Mrs. Smith asked.

"Sure," he answered. "Sure. I watched her

when she hid it. She pinned it over the mantelpiece in the living room."

"Better get ready for bed, Anna," Mr. Smith said.

"I suppose I had better," she said. "But if I thought the girls weren't going to be too late, I'd sort of like to hear what happened."

Grandpa Prophater opened the door to the room where Agnes and Tootie slept. It was cold, and from the light that shone through the door he could see the children's heads against the white pillows. Tootie lay curved into a soft ball and Agnes was on her back, her hands over her head. He reached up to the chandelier and swung the black threads over the glass shades. Then he pulled the figures of the brownies up and went out of the room, slipping the threads under the door before he closed it.

"I hope they won't get too wide awake," Mrs. Smith said. "Not that it matters, I suppose."

The front door opened and closed and Esther and Rose came up the stairs. They were giggling, and they threw themselves on the bed where their father lay, hiding their faces in the blanket to stifle their laughter. Esther's hair was mussed and blown by the wind and Rose had lost some of her dignity. Her pompadour was dishevelled and the three yellow roses she wore in her hair were limp.

Mrs. Smith sat down on the bed beside them. "What happened?" she asked.

They raised their heads. "What didn't happen!" Esther said. "You never saw anything like it when Rose and I made our entrance."

Rose smoothed her hair and pinned the roses tighter. "By the time Lon got there with Lucille Pintard, Esther and I had every dance taken," she said. "And five of my dances were with Harry Jewett, and five of Esther's dances were with Harry Jewett, and as there were only twelve dances and four extras in all, everything went very nicely, thank you."

"I don't know what you're talking about," Mrs. Smith said.

"Suffice it to say that Lon danced with Miss Lucille Pintard to his heart's content and that she agreed to *walk* back to Helen's with him," Esther said.

Mrs. Smith sighed. "It's not that I've got anything against the girl," she said. "I just don't want Lon to take it too hard when she isn't nice to him."

"She isn't so wonderful," Rose said. "She's pretty, if you like her type. She has sort of a rat face, though."

"Decidedly," Esther agreed. "I think Lon is just swept off his feet by her Eastern accent."

"Well, I'm glad to know he had a nice time," Mrs. Smith said softly. "He doesn't have as much money to spend as some of the boys."

"We've decided to arrange her visit for her," Rose said. "Arrange it in much the same way as we arranged it tonight."

Grandpa Prophater came in and turned off the light. "Be quiet, all of you," he said. Then, walking to the door of Agnes' and Tootie's room, he stooped and called through the crack. His voice was high and squeaky. "Agnes and Tootie! Agnes and Tootie!"

There was a rustling from the room and a soft whisper. The children clung together. "It's the Dude," Tootie whispered. "I recognize his voice." They peered into the darkness of the room, and suddenly they saw two small, white figures dancing over the foot of their bed.

"He's got Suspidor with him," Agnes whispered. "I can tell him by his little pointed cap." They pulled the covers up to their chins and shook with excitement.

"Hello, the Dude and Suspidor," Tootie said. "Hello."

"Hello, the Dude and my own darling Suspidor," Agnes said. The figures began to dance more wildly; their small arms and legs whirled in the air. The children's eyes were wide, and their breath came soft and warm from their lips. The brownies made one wild flourish and vanished.

"They've gone," Tootie said. "They came for our notes, and now they've gone."

Agnes sat up, alert as a cat. "I thought I heard sort of a plop on the floor," she said. "I'm going to get out of bed and see if I can find them." She thrust one foot cautiously out of the side of the bed.

Tootie caught the sleeve of her nightgown. "Don't you go! Don't you dare!" she cried. "If you find them and touch them, they'll never come back. Grandpa says so. He says a

December 1903

boy tried to catch one once and the brownies never came again."

Agnes sat on the edge of the bed, swinging her foot. "Maybe there wasn't any brownies," she said. "Brownies don't make any noise, and I heard a sort of plop. Maybe it's just Grandpa playing a joke."

"Don't you go," Tootie said tearfully. "I'll hate you if you go."

Agnes drew her foot back under the covers and moved closer to Tootie. "I won't go," she said. Her voice was comforting and almost mature. "I won't go, Tootie." She lay in the dark, her eyes open, wondering about the brownies and wanting to be sure. When she closed her eyes, she could see the brownies dancing in the air. "Listen, Tootie," she said. "I know it was the brownies. Because I really did see Suspidor's dear little pointed cap."

January 1904

JANUARY 1904

Mrs. Smith came into the living room and stood by the window while she worked her hands into her tight kid gloves. She was dressed entirely in black, and her eyes were red from crying. "It doesn't seem possible that old Mr. Jones almost died and now Mr. Furry has really died," she said. "I can't believe it, somehow."

Grandpa Prophater looked up from the morning paper he was reading. He was seated uncomfortably in a tufted, upholstered chair. The seat was unbending, and three rows of fringe hung down the front, yellow silk fringe generously interwoven with stiff gold thread that pricked his legs when he moved them. It was the most uncomfortable chair in the house and he had chosen it deliberately.

"Now, remember, Father," Mrs. Smith went on, "if you do take Agnes and Tootie to the fairgrounds, see that they wear their rubbers and that you wear *your* rubbers. It will be a mass of mud out there in all this thaw." She looked down at her neat walking shoes. "I ordered a hack. I just couldn't plow through all the slush carrying that big turkey."

"I thought you said Furry was dead," Grandpa Pròphater said.

"Of course he's dead," Mrs. Smith answered sharply.

"Then he won't be much interested in that turkey."

"There are the living to think of, too," his daughter said. She thought of the turkey, browned to a turn and neatly packed in a large box covered with a slightly dampened, clean white napkin. "I mustn't forget to bring the napkin home," she thought. "It's one of my best grape-leaf ones."

"When's that woman going to get out of my room?" Grandpa Prophater asked.

"Miss Thibault will be through the minute she finishes Rose's silk waist," Mrs. Smith said. "She has a good start and she only has the fagoting, the ruching, and the blue ribbons to put on."

"She looks like a pincushion," Grandpa Prophater said.

ST. LOUIS *January 1904*

Mrs. Smith ignored his remark. "And Rose is in her room. And the children are getting dressed," she said. She glanced out the window. "There's the hack." She went to the door to the dining room and called, "Katie, the hack's here! You can bring the turkey!"

Katie appeared through the kitchen door, carrying the box that held the turkey. Her expression was solemn and she wore a black dress under her white kitchen apron. "I'll take it down and put it in myself," she said. "And you might give Mrs. Furry my deepest condolences."

Mrs. Smith sighed. "Well," she said. She stooped and kissed her father lightly on the head, then followed Katie to the front door and down the steps to the street. Grandpa Prophater got up and watched them from the window. He saw them place the box on the seat of the hack and saw that his daughter was being especially careful of her clothes, holding her skirts daintily in one hand as she stepped into the hack and adjusting her veil as Katie shut the door.

Katie stood on the sidewalk, waving, until

the cab was out of sight. Then she walked up the steps briskly and came into the living room. "Esther," she said to Grandpa Prophater, "is deviling the soul out of me for a large pitcher or pail. She says she's got to have it. What'll I tell her?"

"What do I care what you tell her?" he asked.

"Because I won't take the responsibility of anything that Esther has in her mind to do. What does she want a pitcher on a day like this for? What's more, she's taking it out of the house."

Grandpa Prophater turned away from her and once more looked out of the window. The sky was leaden, and streams of water from the melting snow ran in the gutters. The houses, without the vine leaves that covered them from spring to fall, looked commonplace and ugly; the white porches were stained where the drainpipes had rusted and leaked. And all over, the black soot fell day and night from the soft coal that was used in the furnaces. His mind went back to the day when he had heard by rumor, for he was in Andersonville Prison Camp at the time, that his brother Jim had been killed, and of how he had thought Jim was better off dead than sleeping on the cold, hard ground without a blanket to keep him warm. He still carried the picture Jim had had taken when he was made a second lieutenant. It showed Jim standing by an elaborate portière, one hand resting on the back of a carved chair. Jim's trousers were too long and baggy, but his hair was as black and shining as a raven's wing.

He heard Esther as she came through the room. She was dressed in her oldest clothes, a knit cap, and boots, and in her hand she swung a white china pitcher. Her lips were set, but her eyes shone with excitement. Grandpa Prophater was sure she was up to no good.

"You'd think," she said, "that a pitcher was more precious than gold the way you have to try to wangle one out of Katie."

"Katie's a hard, cruel woman," he said.

"Well, she can be *small*. I hate people who are *small*. I don't suppose you could lend me a quarter?" Esther asked.

Grandpa Prophater fished in his vest pocket. "That's a word that gets a lot of use around here," he said. "I'm speaking of the word 'lend.'" He handed her twenty-five cents.

"Oh, thanks heaps," Esther said. "Remind

me, when I get my allowance, that I owe it to you." She slipped the money into her coat pocket and went out the front door. Grandpa Prophater walked slowly toward the stairway. "Might as well polish my sword," he thought. As he went up the stairs he could hear the whirring sound of the sewing machine, and he stopped in the upstairs hall, nerving himself to enter his room, where Miss Thibault, the dressmaker, sat working on Rose's blouse. "Oh, Mr. Prophater, am I in your way?" she asked. She pushed the sewing table an inch or so to one side so that he could pass. The table, which was exactly a yard long, had been nearly ruined by Rose and Esther the year they got their burnt-wood set. On it they had etched pictures of their teachers and expressions they had thought were excruciatingly funny: "Oh you Walter Hoevel!," "Oh you Valentine Party!," "Remember the S.A. Game!"

Suddenly Grandpa Prophater felt that it wouldn't do to take down his sword from the wall. Miss Thibault would make some comment on it and he'd have to answer a lot of damn-fool questions. "Forgot my pipe," he said, and going to his bureau drawer, he took out his pipe and an old Zouave cap that he had brought home from the war as a souvenir. He tucked the cap under his arm and left the room. Crossing the hall, he saw that Rose was in her room sorting papers on her bed, and he stopped, hoping that she was in the mood to stand a bit of teasing. But she only looked up gloomily when she saw him. "Hello, Grandpa," she said. "I'm just getting rid of some Christmas and New Year's stuff. They seem a thousand years away to me now." She laughed bitterly. "Why, just think! I was even excited at going to a dance—just an ordinary dance in this town."

"What are you after now?" he asked.

"I'm not *after* anything at all. Except that there's going to be a big dance, a real dance, at Rolla, and Abbie Gilroy and I aren't sure we're going to be asked." She picked up a piece of cardboard framed in passe-partout. "My New Year's resolutions! When I see how childish they seem!" Her voice rose in an imitation of a child's voice as she read, "'One, to refrain from talking in a loud voice. Two, to refrain from borrowing Esther's or Mamma's personal property, also to refrain from lending

my own. Three, to refrain from sarcasm.'"
Her voice dropped back to normal. "And so
on. It makes me ill to read it."

"I can see how it might," he said. "Why
don't you call up Abbie?"

"I've called her up six times this morning,
and she's called me up about six times. There's
nothing we can do but wait. But we did decide
to destroy everything connected with our pasts.
If we can't have a really exciting future, we
just don't want anything. We've about decided to go to the river together if we can't
go to Rolla."

"I see," Grandpa Prophater said. He
walked slowly into the room Tootie and Agnes
shared. Agnes was sitting on the floor. Beside
her were scissors, paper, and a saucer of flour-and-water paste, and she held a paper doll in
one hand. Tootie had opened the window
slightly and was eating bits of dirty snow from
the window sill. "Don't speak to Agnes," she
said. "Mrs. Van Dusen's head's worn almost
off, and she doesn't want anyone to speak to
her until she gets it fixed. Are we going to the
fairgrounds?"

"Corinne doesn't have to fix *her* paper

dolls," Agnes said. "Corinne is rich and lives in a hotel. They have practically a whole floor to themselves and they order anything they want day and night from a large staff downstairs, who are paid to wait on them hand and foot. Corinne doesn't have to cut her paper dolls out of magazines. She got a whole new set. *Hand-painted* by a real artist. They cost a fortune. They have the dearest little dresses that fasten on, so that she can have the same face for the same person all the time instead of having a different face with every dress. And this was my best Mrs. Van Dusen. And I think I'm going to have to change her name, because Van Dusen is too fancy, and the really rich are unpretentious."

"I'm still going to call my family Rockerfeller," Tootie said. "It sounds so funny. Are we going to the fairgrounds?"

"You two can go where you like," Agnes said. "I'm going to go to see Corinne, and I'm taking the trolley. I'm not going to take my paper dolls, though. I'd be ashamed of them. I will merely say I forgot them."

"Do you really want to go to the fairgrounds, Tootie?" Grandpa Prophater asked.

"It will be all muddy, you know, and there won't be much to see. I don't want you to be disappointed."

"I don't care about the mud," Tootie said.

"It might give you an idea of my old place," Grandpa Prophater said.

Tootie stopped eating snow and looked at him. "What old place?" she asked. "What old place are you talking about? You never had a place as big as the fairgrounds."

Grandpa Prophater slipped the cap from under his arm and put it on his head. "Where do you think this came from?" he asked.

"It came from your room. I've seen it there," Tootie said.

"I didn't ask you where it's *been*," he said. "I asked you where it *came* from."

"Oh," Tootie said. "Where?"

"That's what I'll tell you all about when we see the fairgrounds," he said.

"I don't think it's interesting at all," Agnes said. "Because you've always said you were a poor boy. I'm going to Corinne's. I'm going to order anything I like when they offer me something to eat."

Tootie took her grandfather's hand. Her

own small hand was cold and wet from the snow. "Let's hurry," she said. "I can't bear to wait, can you?"

"No," he said. "I've never been any good at waiting."

It was even muddier at the fairgrounds than they expected. During the summer and fall the grounds had been graded, and now the framework of some of the World's Fair Buildings was finished. Tootie and Grandpa Prophater stood and looked around. "Shall I begin?" he asked.

"Yes," she said.

He pointed to a large area which had been excavated and was now filled with dirty water and small bits of floating ice. "That's where the Lagoon will be," he said. "The water in it will be as blue as the sky and there will be gondolas for people to ride in."

"What are gondolas?" Tootie asked.

"They are little boats," he said. "Not like any boats you've ever seen before. The prows are curved like a swan's throat, and they're paddled by men called gondoliers. Foreign men with black hair, and they sing to you while they take you around. I had a thousand of them once."

"*When?*" Tootie asked. "When did you?"

"When I was a king," Grandpa Prophater said.

Tootie looked up at him and gasped. "You never told me!" she said. "And I've known you all your life."

"It was before you were born," he said. "Before your mother was born. I was only a boy, but I was a real king. I had a lake that was twice as fine as this one, and cascades that were three times as big as the cascades are going to be here. My name was King Fosseque."

"King Fosseque," Tootie repeated. "Where did you live?"

"In a country called Tiaraland. I owned every bit of it. I ate off gold plates, and I ate nothing but the things I liked. Some days I would decide on candy, and candy it would be. Other days I would want nothing but chocolate cake. Or it might be that I expressed a desire for watermelon in midwinter, and fresh watermelon would be brought me by runners from thousands of miles away. Now look to the left of the Lagoon," he said. "Do you see that big space?"

Tootie nodded.

"Well, that's like the place where I kept my griffins. I had a moat built around them so they couldn't escape."

"I know," Tootie said. "They're half lion and half eagle. Lon promised me one once. But he couldn't find one downtown. He looked all afternoon."

Grandpa Prophater laughed. "I could have given you a hundred and never missed them." He took her hand and they started to walk. A few workmen in the first building they passed looked at them as they trudged through the mud. "The reason I was so anxious to have you see the fairgrounds," Grandpa Prophater said, "is because it is going to be almost like my own palace grounds. Only my grounds were bigger, and all the buildings were made of marble and they were set with precious stones."

Slowly they covered every inch of the grounds. It had started to snow lightly and Tootie put out her tongue to catch the flakes as they fell. "I'll like it when all the people come here from all the foreign places," she said. "I want to hear them jabbering away in French."

"It's a strange thing," Grandpa Prophater said, "but I've forgotten most of the language I used to speak. You see, after the war, when I escaped to this country, there were hundreds of spies looking for me, and I didn't dare speak my own tongue. I remember one or two things, though."

Tootie stepped over a puddle. "Tell me one. Just one," she begged.

"Well, *rastoomillia* means hello," he said.

"*Rastoomillia*," Tootie said.

"*Rastoomillia*," her grandfather answered solemnly.

On the way home in the trolley, Tootie barely spoke. Her feet were like ice because the water had seeped in over the tops of her overshoes, but she did not feel them. She had bitten off the tip of one red mitten.

"We're pretty late," Grandpa Prophater said suddenly. He looked at his watch. "It's after five. Your mother's not going to like that."

ST. LOUIS *January 1904*

"What do you care what she thinks?" Tootie asked. "You're a king."

"Well, that makes your mother a princess, and you can't get too gay with them. They're pretty high and mighty."

"If she's a princess, what am I?" Tootie asked.

"You," Grandpa Prophater said, "you'd be a duchess. You see, your mother would have been a queen if she hadn't married your father. He's just a commoner. So one day I made Rose the Queen. One day when she wasn't much older than you are." He looked out the window at the lighted windows of the houses that they passed. "She makes a pretty good queen, too."

He let Tootie ring the bell for the trolley stop, and they got off and started up Kensington Avenue. Near their corner the street was torn up where workmen had been laying a new sewer pipe. Tootie looked at the lanterns that had been lighted and placed near the opening. "I wonder if Ess got to go down into the sewer," she said.

"If she got to do *what*?" Grandpa Prophater asked.

"Go down into the sewer," Tootie repeated. "She was dying to go, and she said she would go if it killed her. The men said they'd let her if she'd bring them a whole lot of beer."

Grandpa Prophater thought of the white pitcher and of Esther's determined mouth. "I wouldn't be surprised if she got to go," he said.

As they went up the steps to their house, Grandpa Prophater put his arm around Tootie. "Of course, you're never to mention about my being a king to anyone outside the house."

"Oh, of course not," Tootie said. "They might find you and kill you."

Inside in the living room, Esther, Agnes, and Mrs. Smith were sitting. Agnes still had her coat on. "And you've never seen people as mean," she was telling her mother indignantly. "They didn't let us order at all, and we had to eat some old mess with plain raisins in it for dessert."

"Raisins are good for you," her mother said. "They have a lot of iron in them."

"I don't care what they have in them," Agnes said, "I *always* pick them out at home, and I couldn't there, because we were in a *restaurant.* If I need iron, I'd just as soon eat rust plain and get it over with."

"Father," Mrs. Smith said, looking at Grandpa Prophater, "where have you been all this time with that child?"

"We went to the fairgrounds," Tootie said. "It's like the place Grandpa used to have, only it's smaller. It is the most beautiful place you ever saw, with a big lagoon, and cascades, and a place especially for griffins."

"As for the paper dolls," Agnes went on, "you'd die. She can't even play with them except for a few minutes. I think I can fix Mrs. Van Dusen."

Tootie took off her stocking cap and shook it. "How was the sewer?" she asked.

"It was nothing but a big pipe," Esther said. "It wasn't even dark. I didn't even see a rat."

Tootie threw her cap on the floor and, reaching up, caught the collar of her grandfather's coat. "I'll help you off with it," she said. She helped him as he pulled his arms through the sleeves, and then she carried the coat to the closet in the back hall and hung it on a hook.

On her way back to the living room, she saw Rose coming down the stairs. "The whole fairgrounds are smaller than King Fosseque's used to be," Tootie said.

"Oh," Rose said, and stopped with one hand on the banister. She felt a pain in her heart, although she spoke casually. "I suppose he made you a queen."

"Of course he didn't," Tootie said. "He made you a queen years ago. I'm a duchess. So's Agnes."

The pain in Rose's heart went away. "Well, Grandpa *was* a king once, and the place is still on the map. I'll show it to you tonight in my atlas. They've changed the name of it now, because they had to. But it's still on the map."

"What's it called now?" Tootie asked.

"It's called Harpers Ferry, West Virginia," Rose answered. "And on the map it's pink."

She took Tootie's hand and they walked into the living room. Rose went over to her grandfather and bowed gracefully. "The Queen," he said.

"Your Majesty," she answered.

"Oh," Mrs. Smith said. She drew Tootie to her. "I was a princess one day when I was your age, or maybe a little younger. It was a rainy Saturday in March when I first heard that I was one." She lifted her eyes and stared into space. "I remember it just as well," she went on. "Because I was sick in bed with the measles, and I was tired of playing with my dolls."

February 1904

FEBRUARY 1904

Agnes and Tootie sat on the bed in their mother's room and watched her as she dressed. She wore a starched white corset cover and a white petticoat with ruffles. She leaned over and started brushing her hair vigorously, drawing the brush from the nape of her neck to the ends of her hair.

"You haven't got so much hair, have you?" Agnes asked. "You should wear a switch. Mrs. Johnson wears a switch. She had it made from her own combings."

"Your father wouldn't hear of it," Mrs. Smith said. She twisted her hair into a soft knot on the top of her head and fastened it with brown bone hairpins. Then she took a box of powder from the top bureau drawer and brushed her face and neck lightly with a soft down puff. "It's only rice powder," she said. "Just so I won't look too shiny. Now, Agnes, if you'll powder my back."

Agnes got up from the bed and took the

puff. "It smells heavenly," she said. "Like violets." She patted her mother's round, pretty shoulders with the puff and smoothed the powder gently over her back.

"And remember," Mrs. Smith said, "you two are to be in bed before the curfew tonight. And mind what Rose tells you. Esther can wash you, Tootie, and Rose can wash Agnes."

"Well," Agnes said. "I must say I'd rather have Esther. At least she washes hard and gets it over with. Rose is awful."

"She's horrible," Tootie agreed. "She gets the washcloth dripping-wet and just pats your face with it. The water runs down all over everything."

"Never mind all that," Mrs. Smith said. "Do as I tell you." She opened her jewel case and took out her diamond earrings.

"Your earrings!" Tootie gasped.

"I'm only wearing them to please your father," Mrs. Smith said. "If you ask me, I think they're a little too showy. Not that this isn't an *occasion*, Mrs. Truman's china wedding."

Tootie's eyes opened wide. "Her China wedding!" She looked at her mother sharply.

ST. LOUIS *February 1904*

"I hope we never have a China wedding in *this* house."

"My china wedding will be in a few months," her mother said. "Not that I intend to make any fuss over it."

Tootie looked horror-stricken. "I think we're all right the way we are." Her eyes filled with tears. "*Every* time we get so we are all right the way we are, somebody wants to butt in. Old buttinskies! What will Papa say?"

"What will Papa say?" her mother asked. "I don't know what you mean. What has Papa *to* say about it? It's a custom, that's all."

"He's the father in this house, isn't he? He's the one who goes to work and brings home all the money. I guess he has a right to say. What are we going to do with Papa? And where are we going to put *him?* He can't have Grandpa's room. Grandpa would go right off his head. Remember how he acted when Rose and Esther burned the incense? What do you think he's going to say when there's nothing but incense around here? Besides, I couldn't tell Helen Ferris. She'd die."

"Couldn't tell her *what?*" Mrs. Smith asked.

"Couldn't tell her that you had to marry a Chinaman," Tootie said.

Mrs. Smith leaned against the bureau and laughed. "Tootie, Tootie," she said. "I'm not going to marry a Chinaman. A china wedding is a sort of celebration that you give on your wedding anniversary when you have been married a number of years. And all your friends give you china."

"Oh," Tootie said. "Then I'll save my money and buy you something made of china. I would rather be poor than have you getting rid of Papa. I've liked him ever since he came into this family."

Mrs. Smith went to the closet and took out a dress. It was carefully covered with an old sheet, and the two little girls knew it was the dress Aunt Emma had sent their mother from Paris. It was made of shell-pink satin covered with black lace.

"Can I hook you up in it this time?" Tootie asked.

Mrs. Smith stepped into the dress so as not to muss her hair. "I think Agnes better do it," she said. "She's older and her little fingers are quicker than yours." Agnes shot Tootie a triumphant glance and set to work on the innumerable hooks and eyes. While her dress was being fastened, Mrs. Smith fished in the bureau drawer and brought out a pink lipstick enclosed in shiny cardboard. She looked at it dubiously for a moment, then began to use it lightly. "My lips chap so," she murmured. When the dress was fastened she stood back and looked at herself in the mirror. She looked young, pretty, and shining. "Now, Tootie," she said, "you can open the Jicky bottle."

Tootie got down from the bed and walked over to the bureau. There was something ceremonial in the way she handled the perfume bottle and took out the glass stopper. Her mother touched the stopper lightly to her dress and hair. And then, tipping the bottle, holding her finger over the opening until it was wet with perfume, she brushed it lightly through Agnes's soft brown hair. Tootie stood silently by until her mother, repeating the familiar action, ran her hand through her short curls.

Agnes rubbed her head against her mother's dress. "I wish you looked this way all the time," she said.

There were steps in the upstairs hall and a knock at the door. "Come in," Mrs. Smith called. The door opened and Mr. Smith and Grandpa Prophater came in. They were in full evening dress and carried top hats folded under their arms. They looked at Mrs. Smith admiringly, and she turned away, straightening the things on her bureau so that they wouldn't notice that she was blushing.

"The hack is here, Annie," Grandpa Prophater said.

"I'm ready," she said. The others stood aside as she swept from the room, her skirts rustling, her earrings sparkling.

Mr. Smith, breathing in the smell of Jicky as she passed, noticed the house dress that she had worn all day hanging across the back of a chair. It was a dull thing and he snatched it from the chair and, opening the closet, threw it rudely on the floor. "Damn it all," he said. Then he followed his wife down the stairs.

Grandpa Prophater took Agnes and Tootie by the hand. "It's a fine thing to be rich," he said.

They looked at him with bright, shining eyes. "Oh, yes!" they said.

When Grandpa Prophater and the two children reached the downstairs hall, Mrs.

Smith, her sealskin cape thrown around her shoulders, was saying to Rose and Esther, "And remember, just because we are all going out and it's Katie's day off, you are not to run wild. I don't want to see any of the boys here when we get home, even if tomorrow is Saturday. And you don't have to feed those boys until they burst. They've had their dinner and all they will want is a little light supper. How many are coming?"

"Six," Esther said. "And we won't be making any noise, because we are merely going to run through the score of 'Cavalleria Rusticana.'"

"Run through it?" Rose said. "Why, we haven't gotten past the Siciliana. And we're just going to feed them welsh rarebit and some pickles, candy, dates, and cider. And we thought, if you didn't mind, we might make some pralines in the chafing dish."

"Very well," Mrs. Smith said.

Mr. Smith looked at his watch. "It's after eight," he said.

Mrs. Smith gave a frantic look at her four girls. "I don't like to go and leave you all alone," she said.

Agnes's eyes slowly filled with tears. "Goodbye," she said, hugging her mother wildly.

Mrs. Smith stooped and whispered in her ear. "I'll bring you something. Decorated mints or some little thing."

"Here," Esther said. "Here's the vase. I bet nobody else will bring such a lovely present. Ten dollars is a *lot* for a vase."

As her father, mother, and grandfather moved toward the door, Tootie began to sing loudly:

Brighten the corner where you are,
Brighten the corner where you are,
Someone far from Harvard you can guide across
  the bar,
Brighten the corner where you are.

"Don't let her keep on that way," Mrs. Smith said. "She gets much too excited."

The four girls stood with their arms around one another as they watched their parents and Grandpa Prophater get into the hack. "Two horses," Agnes said. "They've got two horses. Don't they look *stylish*!" They watched until the hack passed up the street and out of sight. Then Esther turned briskly. "Now, you two," she said. "You can begin getting ready for bed."

"I'm going to stay up until *just* before the curfew." Tootie said firmly. "Mamma told me simply to be in bed before the curfew."

"So am I," Agnes said.

"Look," Rose said. "Suppose you get undressed, and Esther and I will light a lovely fire in the gas grate, and after we wash you we'll bring you up something to eat."

"What?" Agnes asked.

Rose looked meaningly at Esther. "Some fudge," she said. "And some stuffed dates and some cider."

"I like welsh rarebit," Tootie said. She moved closer to Agnes and set her mouth.

"Don't be utterly absurd," Esther said. "We won't even begin to make the Welsh rarebit until you're sound asleep."

"I can't promise to go to sleep," Agnes said. "Remember the time Mamma went downtown all day and I sat on the front steps waiting for her?"

"I remember," Rose said. Her voice was

grim. "And I also remember that you got a good whaling for it."

Agnes looked thoughtfully at a spot over Rose's head and then turned to face Tootie. "I'll tell you what we can do," she said. "We can go up and get ready for bed. We can even get in bed."

They walked upstairs arm in arm. As they went into their room, they heard the doorbell ring and the sound of voices.

"It's George Briggs and Alex Harper and that horrible Fred," Agnes said. "Let's look over the banisters when that Fred begins to act foolish." She sat down on the floor and started to unbutton her shoes.

Tootie walked toward the mantelpiece and took a match from a container. She scraped it across the trousers of the figure of a Dutch boy. The body of the figure was made of gaily painted tin, but the trousers were made of sandpaper, and across the upper part of them there was a verse, which read:

> *Don't scratch matches on the walls,*
> *Scratch them on my overalls.*

"Let's scratch a lot of matches before we turn on the gas grate," Tootie said.

ST. LOUIS *February 1904*

Agnes stood up in her stocking feet and took a handful of matches. For a while she and Tootie lighted match after match and watched as the flame flared up and burned dangerously near their fingers. Their movements were slow and deliberate, as though they were hypnotized. Finally, Agnes sighed. "I suppose we'd better light the grate now," she said.

Tootie turned the handle and Agnes held a match to one of the slits in the asbestos. A small, blue flame showed and then, in a burst, the entire grate glowed blue and yellow. The two children sat down in front of it and pulled off their clothes. When they were naked they sat with their backs to the fire, their arms folded around their knees. After a while Agnes got up, walked across the room, and looked at Tootie's doll, which was lying in its carriage. "I tell you what," she said, "Margaretha might get galloping consumption."

"She could," Tootie agreed. "But not bad."

"No, not bad," Agnes said. "Just bad enough to wrap her up all warm and put her in a box and hang her out the window by a string."

Downstairs the doorbell rang again, and

Agnes and Tootie could hear a louder sound of voices now. They took Margaretha from her carriage, and Tootie felt her head. "She's burning up," she said.

"We'd better get her in the box quick," Agnes said. "I've got a box. We can punch holes in the top so she'll get plenty of good, fresh air."

They undressed Margaretha tenderly and wrapped her in bits of soft flannel and laid her in the box, which Agnes pulled out from under the bed. Then, fastening a string around the box, they lowered it carefully down from the window until it bumped gently against the top of the living-room window.

"I guess she'll be worse tomorrow," Tootie said. "And we'll have to do something more."

Hearing the sound of the piano below, Tootie and Agnes opened their door and stood listening in the doorway. Esther was singing:

Oh, Lola, with thy cheeks redder than berries,
Brow with a flush ever more glowing,
Lips that were made to kiss like ripening cherries,
Thanks should be given to Heaven for their be-
  stowing.

ST. LOUIS *February 1904*

"Do you like it?" Agnes asked.

"Yes, I like it," Tootie said. "I can sing it, too. Let's creep down halfway and look at them."

"I think we should put on our nightgowns, just in case," Agnes said.

Slipping their nightdresses over their heads, they tiptoed softly to the stair landing. Rose sat at the piano, and standing beside her was Esther, a red bow in her black hair. Her head was thrown back and her dimples showed as she sang. The hall was filled with pipe smoke, and six young men were sitting on the floor around the piano.

George Briggs was the first to hear the creaking of the stairs. He looked up toward the landing and cleared his throat. "Miss Rose," he said, "there are mice in this house. Two of them."

Rose turned abruptly on the piano stool. "Tootie and Agnes!" she cried. "I forgot all about them. They're supposed to be in bed."

"Well, as long as they aren't in bed, they might as well come down," George said.

Agnes and Tootie gave delighted screams and ran down the stairs.

"They're in their nightgowns," Esther gasped. "Really!"

"So they are," Alex Harper agreed.

Tootie ran quickly to George Briggs and caught his arm. "I want to sing, too," she said.

"Very well, dear," Rose said calmly. She turned to George with a little shrug. "She sings quite sweetly, you know. What would you like to sing, Tootie? 'Baby's Boat's the Silver Moon' or 'Have You Ever Seen a Rabbit Climb a Tree?'"

Agnes edged in between Alex Harper and the hall table, on which sat a platter of fudge. She reached up and took four pieces.

"I don't like those songs," Tootie said. "I'm tired of them. I think I'll sing a song Lon taught me. He learned it at Princeton. And he taught it to me when he came home for Christmas. I've never sung it here before. Just for some people on the street once."

"Well, you can't sing it," Rose said flatly. "I don't know the music."

"I can sing it without the music," Tootie said. "I always have."

"I don't think you'd better, Tootie dear," Rose said. "Now that you've seen George, why don't you and Agnes run upstairs? Esther and I will be right up to wash your faces and tuck you in your bed." She smiled at George. "Our maid is out, you know."

"And we'll bring you up a nice little supper," Esther said. "And you can eat it in *bed*. Won't that be fun?"

"The song begins 'I was *hmm* last night, dear mother,'" Tootie said.

The young men laughed. "Go on, Tootie," George said. "Get up and sing it loud. It seems to me I've heard it before."

"Well, I haven't," Rose said. "And I wouldn't encourage her if I were you. There are times when she gets as bold as brass and there's no stopping her."

Tootie moved away from George and stood in the space between the portières that hung in the doorway to the living room. She bowed and for a moment looked frightened. But when she began to sing everything went out of her head but the tune and the words of the song she sang:

> *I was drunk last night, dear mother.*
> *I was drunk the night before.*
> *But if you'll forgive me, Mother,*
> *I'll never get drunk any more.*

Rose and Esther stared at her, stunned. Agnes let the fudge dissolve slowly in her mouth and looked at Tootie with admiration. Then Esther ran and picked up Tootie in her arms. "You bad girl!" she cried. "You bad girl!" She began to laugh. "It's really Lon's fault," she said to Rose.

Agnes got up and pushed her way toward Tootie. "I can dance," she said. "I can do the cakewalk."

"And I can play it," Rose said. She turned the piano stool around again.

"Here, give her my hat," Fred Raleigh said.

Agnes stood beating time to the music with her bare feet, and then, throwing the upper part of her body backward, she twirled the hat in her hand and stepped out stiffly across the room.

George Briggs leaned over Rose's shoulders as she played. "They're smart, those two," he said.

Rose turned to look at Agnes as she strutted back and forth across the room. "I suppose they are," she said.

It was almost half past ten, and Tootie had

sung her entire repertoire of songs and Agnes had danced until her hair was moist with perspiration, when Rose led them upstairs. "I was drunk last night, dear mother!" Tootie shouted when she reached the landing, and was gratified by a round of applause.

"Here," Rose said. "Just run in and wash your own faces with plain water, and we'll be up with some food."

In the bathroom, Agnes let the water run slowly over her hands and Tootie patted her face with a damp washcloth. Then they went into their own room, which was hot from the fire in the gas grate. They kneeled down to say their prayers. "I think I'll say all my prayers," Tootie said. "I think I'll say 'Hail Mary,' 'Our Father,' and 'Now I Lay Me.'"

"I'll just say 'Our Father,'" Agnes said. "I've had a good enough time. I think I better save the others until I really need them. If you say them every day, all of them, you haven't anything for extra when you want something." She clasped her hands and looked up to the ceiling. The soles of her feet were dirty, but her face was pure and delicate. Tootie bowed her head.

"Don't do that," Agnes said sharply. "Lon

says when you bow your head, you're praying to the Devil. You have to keep your eyes up to Heaven."

As the two little girls finished their prayers, Esther came into the room with two plates. Three small pickles, three stuffed dates, a piece of fudge, and a glass of cider were on each plate. "Now eat this and go to sleep," she said. "We have to make the Welsh rarebit and get the boys out of here before Papa and Mamma show up. You can't tell. They might come home early." She turned off the gas grate and went out, closing the door behind her.

"While we eat," Tootie said, "tell me a story."

Agnes bit into a pickle. It tasted fresh and sharp after the fudge she had eaten. "All right," she said. "Once upon a time there was a madman. Now, first I have to explain that the only way you can keep a madman quiet is to look him straight in the eyes and sing to him. . . ."

At a quarter to twelve the boys said goodbye, and Esther and Rose carried the used plates into the kitchen. "Imagine, George giving me his cute little fraternity pin," Rose said. "I'm going to pin it to my fob with the others."

"I don't know when I've had such a good time," Esther said. "I'm still cold with joy."

Agnes, hearing the front door close, climbed out of bed and went to the head of the back stairs. "Rose!" she called. "Tootie can't get to sleep."

"Can't get to sleep!" Rose exclaimed. "What are *we* going to do?"

"I don't know," Agnes said. "I've been telling her stories and telling her stories, and she just can't go to sleep."

"Did you bounce her in bed?" Esther asked. "That usually does it."

"Yes," Rose said. "I think we'd better go up and bounce her before Mamma gets home."

They ran up the stairs and Agnes led the way into the bedroom, where Tootie was sitting up in bed, bright-eyed. "Now I'm going to turn off the light, Tootie," Esther said, "and you lie down and we'll bounce you a little." Agnes crept back into bed and Esther sat at the foot, shaking the bed gently.

"You'd better do it harder," Agnes said.

"When you do it a little bit, she gets sick. But if you bounce her hard enough to send her up in the air, she gets tired and goes to sleep."

"All right," Rose said. She leaned over the bed, her hands resting on the side of the mattress. "Here we go!"

At the first bounce, Tootie's small body shot up in the air. She gasped and began to laugh a little hysterically. As Rose and Esther bounced her harder, they giggled and panted. And every now and then one of them would fall across the bed, gasping for air. Then suddenly Tootie cried, "Rose! I think I'm going to be sick!"

In a flash, Rose had grabbed her and carried her to the bathroom. A little later, Rose came back into the bedroom with Tootie, pale and exhausted, in her arms. Esther smoothed the bed and Rose laid Tootie down gently.

"It's funny," Agnes said. "I feel fine."

"I feel fine, too," Tootie said. "It was only for a while I didn't."

Down the street they heard the sound of horses' hoofs. "They're coming!" Rose cried. "Quick! Close your eyes! And we'll go into our room and shut the door. Thank Heaven, *our* light isn't on."

The house was very still when Mrs. Smith came in the front door. "Well," she said. "They're actually in bed."

"They left the lights on," Grandpa Prophater said. He started to turn them off, one by one.

Mrs. Smith opened the door to the kitchen and glanced in. "They didn't wash the dishes," she said. "I really think I should clean up and not leave that mess for Katie in the morning."

"Come to bed, Anna, and stop fussing," Mr. Smith said. He put his arm around her and they walked up the stairs and tiptoed across the hall to their own room.

Grandpa Prophater went into the kitchen and shuddered at what he saw. Pans stood soaking in the sink and a few dishes were set carelessly on the kitchen table. As he reached up to turn out the light, there was a ring at the doorbell. It was a steady, urgent ring.

Upstairs, Mrs. Smith started. "Who can that be at this hour of the night?" she said.

"I hope there's been no accident." She opened the door leading into the hall and listened. "Father's talking to someone. Why, it sounds like Mr. Trask, the night watchman!"

Mr. Smith came over and stood beside her. He had taken off his coat and trousers. They waited nervously until Grandpa Prophater came up the stairs. He carried a box, a candy box, with holes punched in the top.

"Why, what is it?" Mrs. Smith asked.

"Trask saw the box hanging from the upstairs window," Grandpa Prophater said. "He thought it might be a sneak thief lowering his loot down to a pal. He climbed up on the window sill and took the box down. And when we opened it, we found *this*." He held the box out toward them and lifted the top. They all stared down at Margaretha, who lay peacefully, with her wax eyelids closed.

Mrs. Smith walked across the hall and went into the children's room. Agnes's and Tootie's eyes were closed and their breathing was regular. She tucked the covers in at the side of their bed and tiptoed out again. "I can't imagine what made them do that," she said. "Tootie loves Margaretha. She usually wants to sleep with her. And their room is so warm that it smells funny."

Grandpa Prophater set the box down on his daughter's bed. "Well, Annie," he said, "I gave Trask a dollar for his trouble."

"You shouldn't have done that, Father," Mrs. Smith said. "After all, we do *pay* him to watch the house."

Grandpa Prophater's eyes were bright. "I've always found it expedient to keep on the right side of the police," he said.

March 1904

MARCH 1904

Rose reached up to take the hatpins out of her hat. Her pompadour had parted in the middle, which gave her a rather dishevelled look, and one of her gloves had split across the palm. Her mother waited until she had thrown her hat, coat, and gloves on a chair in the living room before she spoke. "Well?" she asked.

"Well," Rose said. "In the first place, we saw everybody we knew, and I'd give ten farms to do it all over again. And you can't believe what that grand-looking Paul Hendricks said about me, and also what Mr. Barnard said. But he's married, so it doesn't count."

"And where's Esther?" Mrs. Smith asked.

"She stopped to get a cherry phosphate," Rose answered. "We had two sundaes at Plow's after the matinée, and she felt a little funny on the trolley coming home. So she thought she'd get a cherry phosphate to sort of settle her stomach." She sat down on a small, straight chair and pushed her hair back from her forehead. "If I ever write," she said, "I hope I can think of a title as wonderful as 'A Gilded Fool.'"

Mrs. Smith picked up the coat, hat, and gloves from the chair. "How was Nat Goodwin?" she asked.

"Oh, he was wonderful, too," Rose said. "We are *much* for him."

Her mother stood holding the wraps, and Rose, looking directly at her, saw that she seemed excited.

"What are you two girls doing tonight?" Mrs. Smith asked.

"Tonight?" Rose repeated. "Well, tonight we were going to fool around with Lon and some friends of his. Why?"

Mrs. Smith drew herself up and lifted her chin in the air. "Do what you like, of course," she said. "But Mrs. Wagner called, and she has extended a very unusual invitation to you, Esther, and myself. It seems that she has made the acquaintance of Mme. Roditi, the little Frenchwoman who has come on for the World's Fair. She's going to be quite a factor in the French Pavilion. And Mme. Roditi is giving an at-home this evening for the Chinese Commissioner's wife."

"An at-home!" Rose said. "I wouldn't miss it for anything."

"That's what I thought," her mother said. "So Katie has your dresses pressed, and we'll have a light supper. There's to be a German Countess there, too. I called your father and he said he'd eat downtown."

Tootie came into the room and stood braiding the tassels of the portières. "If you're talking about that at-home," she said, "Papa won't go, because he has no use for foreigners. He has no use for English people, French people, or any people at all. He says he doesn't understand them and he doesn't want to."

"Your father doesn't show much sense at times," Mrs. Smith said.

"Grandpa won't go, either," Tootie said. "And I asked Katie if she would if she had a chance, and she said not on your life. Agnes says she wouldn't go unless she was taken there by a governess, but I would just as soon go, if you'd let me, because I like to hear people talk crazy."

"Leave those portières alone," Mrs. Smith said. She leaned forward and slapped Tootie's hands sharply.

"Listen, Tootie," Rose said. "Just because

people don't speak the same language you do is no reason why they talk crazy."

"The Chinese laundryman at the corner talks crazy," Tootie said. "Every time I yell at him he goes right out of his head. I wouldn't be surprised if he came at me with a knife one of these days."

The front door opened and closed and Esther hurried into the room. "I met Mrs. Wagner and she told me," she said. "She said Mme. Roditi has the queerest place, all wonderful and foreign. She rented the Barneses' house, but Mrs. Wagner says you'd never know it ever *belonged* to them. She's moved their furniture out into the carriage house and has moved loads and loads of her own things in. Mrs. Wagner says her curtains are a dream, and she keeps them pulled to all day, so that hardly an ounce of light ever gets in. And it's just as mysterious."

Tootie shook her head. "Her bills will be awful," she said. "I suppose she hasn't thought about *them*." She turned and started to leave the room when suddenly she stopped and looked down at her hands. The backs of them were still pink where her mother had slapped them. "You didn't hurt me," she said. "I hardly felt it." Then, as her mother made a quick move in her direction, she darted across the hall and up the stairs.

Agnes was sitting on the stairs that led to the third floor. Beside her she had a small stack of paper bags. "I'm fixing these to play a joke on Lon and those boys tonight," she told Tootie. "When they come and get to acting smart, I'm going to fill these with water and drop them on their heads. You can help me."

"Where are you going to drop them *from*?" Tootie asked.

"Well, I can't quite make up my mind," Agnes said. "I thought we might drop them from the window in the girls' room and hit them as they came in. But then I thought one of them might tell the other, or yell out, or something. And the whole thing would be ruined. So I think we had better just throw them from the landing."

"What'll Mamma say about all that water?" Tootie asked.

"Oh, *her*!" Agnes said. "She'll be too excited to notice the water when she gets home. Anyway, Grandpa said he'd help us clean up. He's disgusted with Mamma and the girls."

"Anybody can talk Chinese," Tootie said. "Velly fine. I would like to hear Rose putting on like that." She pulled a strand of hair down over her forehead and wrapped it around the tip of her nose. Then she pulled the lower lids of her eyes down until they showed red and stuck her tongue out.

Agnes smoothed the bags neatly. "That's your best face," she said.

"I know," Tootie said. "I suppose that Mme. Roditi thinks she's making a palace out of the Barneses' house. She'll probably want to dig a moat."

From below they heard the sound of the dinner bell, and almost immediately Grandpa Prophater's door opened and he came out into the hall. "We're in for it," he said. "A lot of fool nonsense. I don't know what's got into your mother lately. She can't seem to stay home, where she belongs. Wanting to run around with a lot of heathens, and then doing the Stations of the Cross every Sunday to make up for it."

ST. LOUIS *March 1904*

"Grandpa," Tootie said thoughtfully, "if it will make you feel any better, Agnes and I can go down and yell at the Chinaman at the corner after dinner."

"You'll do nothing of the sort," he said. "You stay home, where you belong. It's more than the rest of them do."

"I'll bet Papa's mad," Agnes said. "I can't just imagine how he feels with his wife and daughters going out alone and meeting a lot of strangers."

Grandpa Prophater smoothed his mustache. "He ought to put his foot down," he said.

"I never saw Papa put his foot down," Tootie said. She took her grandfather's hand and started down the stairs. Agnes got up and smoothed the skirt of her Peter Thomson suit before she followed them. She waited until they were at the foot of the stairs and then sang softly to herself, "Ching Ching Chinaman, eat dead rats. Chew them up like gingersnaps."

That evening the carriage in which Rose and Esther sat facing their mother and Mrs.

Wagner pulled up short about half a block from Mme. Roditi's house and fell in the line, which moved slowly to the porte-cochère. The carriage lamps looked blurred and dim in the fog.

Esther moved uneasily and her knees hit against Mrs. Wagner's dress. "Oh, I *beg* your pardon," she said.

"*Pas de tout*," Mrs. Wagner said. She gave a bright little laugh. "You see, I'm speaking French already, and we're not even *there*."

"I'm frantic about my French, even though I got a B-plus in it," Rose said.

"Think of me," Mrs. Smith said. "I don't know a word of it, except a few little things I remember from one of the French sisters in the convent."

Their carriage stopped under the porte-cochère, and Esther twisted her hands nervously. The coachman got down from his box and opened the door, and they stepped out daintily. Their heels clicked on the moist wooden stairs that led to the front door. Inside, the house was softly lighted, and they walked up the stairway to leave their wraps in a second-floor bedroom. On the bed was a pile of capes and balloon-sleeved coats. The bedspread was made of pink brocaded satin, and Mrs. Smith stood looking down at it. "This never belonged to Hetty Barnes," she said. "I suppose it's *hers*."

"Mamma!" Rose said in a whisper. "You've simply got to pretend not to notice such things. After all, we don't want her to think we're not *used* to the best."

Mrs. Smith untied the black lace scarf which she had worn over her head. "She'll find out soon enough without my telling her," she said. "She'll find out after she returns a few calls. And I must say that I think satin is entirely out of place on a *bed*. It can't be washed."

Esther and Rose threw their capes across the top of the pile. "I never saw such a *pink* room," Esther said. She looked around. "*Too* pink."

"I think she's overdone it a little," Rose agreed. Now that she was in the house it had lost some of its terror for her. She walked nonchalantly to the pier glass and patted her hair. "We might as well go down."

The living room was crowded with people. Mme. Roditi stood at the head of the receiving line, and at her left were a black-haired Chinese woman and a blonde woman, almost six feet tall, whose clothes looked as though an inexpensive upholsterer had fitted her into them.

"Look," Mrs. Wagner said. "The tall one is the German Countess."

"Very elegant, I suppose, for wherever she's from," Mrs. Smith said. "But not the thing, not the thing *at all*, for St. Louis."

"The first time I met her," Mrs. Wagner said, "she slouched in her chair. But I must admit she could converse interestingly in French, English, German, and, I suppose, really, any language if the opportunity had presented itself."

A group of people were slowly making their way to the receiving line, and Mrs. Wagner motioned Mrs. Smith, Rose, and Esther to join them. The room was strangely silent considering the number of people in it, although there seemed to be a lessening of tension once the introductions were over. Parties had gathered in groups; five young Chinese stood by themselves, some elegant Frenchmen stood alone, and the St. Louis people gathered in sets and looked around at the curtains, the paintings, and into the dining room, where a buffet-supper table had been set. Mrs. Smith felt as though she were in a dream. She heard Mrs. Wagner say, "And here, dear Mme. Roditi, is Mrs. Smith and her two lovely daughters, Miss Rose and Miss Esther."

Mrs. Smith took Mme. Roditi's hand and looked at her for the first time. Mme. Roditi was a short, dark woman with a wide, blunt nose. Her eyes were very black and darted around Mrs. Smith without once seeming to see her. Mrs. Smith withdrew her hand. "I wouldn't trust her as far as I could throw a cow by the tail," she thought. She passed on, touching the fragile hand of the pretty Chinese woman and acknowledging the introduction to the dreadful Countess.

After the Smiths got through the receiving line, Mrs. Wagner led them across the room to the group of young Chinese. She patted the arm of one of them, and he turned around. "Mr. Feng Hsu," she said. "Mr. Feng Hsu, here are the two charming young ladies I was speaking of." She smiled at Rose and Esther. "Mr. Feng Hsu," she said, "is going to give a lecture here next week on 'Courtship and Marriage in China.' And *I* told him that you might give him some ideas of *courtship* in America."

Rose looked down at him through her lashes. He was slightly smaller than she was and his skin was the color of ivory. As she looked into his eyes she saw that he was laughing at her. "We will listen to it with all our ears," she said.

"That will be kind of you, *Mademoiselle*," he said.

"Here we are called Miss," she told him. "And you will have to speak slowly at your lecture so that we can all understand you, because, naturally, we are thrilled."

"I think," he said, "that the Chinese grasp American humor."

Mrs. Wagner looked nervously at Rose, and surreptitiously tugged at her sleeve. Rose moved away from her slowly and deliberately.

"And I would like to know," Mr. Feng Hsu said, "why you say fall in love. Why don't you say rise to love?"

Esther laughed. "That's very good," she said.

ST. LOUIS *March 1904*

Rose looked at her, and then laughed too. "It *was* good," she said, and her voice was warm.

"And now," Mr. Feng Hsu said, "I would like to present you to my friends, Mr. Wu, Mr. Yen Wang, Mr. Chiang Paotzu, and Mr. Kuo Chang." Rose and Esther nodded their heads graciously.

"Well, now," Mrs. Wagner said, "now that you seem to be having such a pleasant time together, I'm going to take your mother away. I always think that children get along better by themselves."

The group of young people stood silently for a while. Then Esther spoke. "Rose and I thought that you'd wear your national costume," she said.

The men laughed. "You are in school?" Mr. Kuo Chang asked. "Where do you go to school?"

"Oh, at Mary Institute, of course," Rose said. "I'm a senior and Esther's a junior. We have a brother named Lon, who's at Princeton. And we have two younger sisters. One's twelve. That's Agnes. And one's six. That's Tootie."

"Our grandfather lives with us, too," Esther said. "And our maid's name is Katie."

"Oh?" Mr. Kuo Chang said.

"Yes," Rose said. "We are a large family."

"And all so pretty?" Mr. Wu asked.

Rose blushed. "We are considered to be," she said.

"Rose has seven or eight fraternity pins," Esther said. "There's not another girl in town that has that many."

"Eight," Rose corrected her. "I have one DKE. That stands for Delta Kappa Epsilon. Two SAE pins, one Beta, and four others. The others don't count much."

"They count some," Esther said.

"Well, maybe," Rose admitted. "But the most important member in our family is Lon. He's home for Easter vacation now. He'll be a sophomore at Princeton next year, and probably leader of the mandolin club. He plays the mandolin beautifully. And he's a mile runner, besides."

"And he must be very proud of his sisters," Mr. Wu said.

"Oh, he is," Esther said. "Why, he took our pictures away with him to Princeton and they caused a sensation. Now, you must tell us something about yourselves."

The young men looked at one another and then looked at Rose and Esther. "We have nothing that will compare with your stories," Mr. Feng Hsu said.

Esther shook her head and sighed. "I suppose not. I really think that more happens to our family than to any family in the world. I mean, for instance, today we went to the matinée and tonight we are here. And right in our house, this very minute, there are a dozen boys. Heaven knows what they're doing. And there's always something doing. Tootie breaks her arm a lot, and my Grandfather is a very interesting man who fought in the Civil War. I suppose you've read about the Civil War? And then there's the World's Fair coming, which *of course* you know about. And—" She caught her breath. "Well, you can see how it goes."

Mr. Feng Hsu looked at the two girls. They seemed to him very young and alien. And he didn't know what they were talking about.

Rose smiled at him. "Do you mind if I ask you a very rude question?" she asked.

"Not at all," he said.

She looked over her shoulder and nodded toward the Countess. "Well, you see that Countess there," she said. "Now this is very rude, but I would appreciate awfully if you would answer me directly and truthfully no matter how it sounds. Do you honestly think that in any country she would be considered even passable? I mean, don't you think she's actually ugly?"

Mr. Feng Hsu glanced at the Countess. "Yes, I think so," he said.

"And don't you think," Rose went on, "that her clothes look as though they were of the vintage of ninety-two?"

"They are strange, indeed," Mr. Feng Hsu said.

Rose nodded at him, and Esther giggled. Then they all began to laugh. "Really, that was dreadful of me," Rose said. "But now we have something in common."

A waiter passed by with a tray loaded with glasses. Rose touched him lightly on the arm. "Would you like some punch, Mr. Feng Hsu?" she asked. "Or *voulez-vous du thé*?"

It was after one when the party broke up.

ST. LOUIS *March 1904*

Rose and Esther were silent during the drive home, but as they started up the steps to their front porch, Rose said, "Ess, I'm just zizzy for everything Chinese, aren't you? I don't see why we can't fix up our room with joss sticks and vases and idols, do you?"

"You'll have no idols," Mrs. Smith said. As she took out her key she noticed that there was a light still burning in the dining room. She opened the door and saw that the hall floor was damp. She walked through the living room into the dining room, where Mr. Smith and Grandpa Prophater sat at the table playing cribbage. She walked around the table and kissed her husband lightly on the cheek.

"Well," he said. "Have a good time, Anna?"

"I wouldn't say I had a good time, exactly," Mrs. Smith said. "It was an odd kind of time. The girls got along very nicely with some young men, but I can't say I cottoned to Mme. Roditi. She's a slinky sort. And the food wasn't so much considering the way she's fixed up Mrs. Barnes' house, as though it wasn't good enough for anybody in the first place."

Rose and Esther pulled two chairs close to the table and sat down. "We loved it," Rose said. "Slanting eyes, jet-black hair, and all."

Grandpa Prophater moved a white ivory peg on the board. "Funny thing happened here," he said. "For some reason, Agnes and Tootie went down to the corner after dinner and began to yell at that Chinaman who has the laundry. He chased them with a flatiron. At least, that's what they said."

"The idea!" Mrs. Smith said. "You'll have to go down and speak to him. After all, they are just little girls and they don't mean any harm. You speak to him and I'll speak to them. I'll forbid them to go near him."

"I spoke to him," Mr. Smith said. "He just laughed and gave me a bag of nuts to take to them. From what I could understand, he was just having fun with them."

"Well, don't give them the nuts," Mrs. Smith said. "Goodness knows where he got them. They might poison the children if they ate them."

"They've eaten them," Mr. Smith said. "And I went up about ten minutes ago and they were still alive."

"Yes," Grandpa Prophater said. "They were alive. They weren't even asleep."

April 1904

APRIL 1904

Mr. Smith got off the trolley and turned down Kensington Avenue. Under one arm he carried a box of Peter Oak's candy and the evening paper. He walked more quickly than usual, and his lips moved as he talked silently to himself. He ran up the cement steps to the terraced lawn of his home and waited a few minutes before he went up the wooden steps that led to the front porch. He stood fumbling with his key ring, then, picking out the key to the front door, he stared at it for a few moments and then ran his fingers along its smooth, worn surface. He had been opening the front door with it for almost twenty-one years.

There was no one in the hall as he entered. The top of the piano was piled high with music and there was a jardinière filled with pussy willows on the hall table. Although the door that led into the back hall was shut, he could hear his wife and Katie moving about in the kitchen, brisk and efficient. He wondered what they would do about Katie. "Anna!" he called. He took off his coat and hat and laid them across the piano stool.

The door to the back hall opened and Mrs. Smith hurried out. "Goodness, Lonnie!" she said. "You startled me." She looked at the candy box under his arm and said, "*More* candy!"

He handed the box to her without speaking and, putting his arm around her waist, walked with her into the living room. "Where are the girls?" he asked.

Mrs. Smith stared at him. "What's the matter?" she asked. "How should I know where the girls are?"

"Well, I just wanted to talk to you alone for a minute," he answered. He sat down in a chair by the mantelpiece and sighed. "Now, Anna," he said, "don't fly up in the air. There's nothing to lose your head over. I know it will be a lot of work for you and a lot of upset. But in the end it will be the wise thing."

"What will be the wise thing?" Mrs. Smith asked. "I don't know what you're talking about. Now, see here, Lonnie, I'm as calm as a cucumber. And you're shaking like I don't know what."

He held out his hand and she took it. "Well, I haven't mentioned it before," he said, "but there's been some talk downtown lately about sending me to New York. And today it was decided that they would send me."

Mrs. Smith laughed. "Well, we can live without you for a while," she said, patting his hand. "Only I hope you won't have to stay so long that you'll miss the opening of the World's Fair."

Mr. Smith held her hand tightly. "You don't understand," he said. "I mean they're sending me to New York for good. To be the head of the New York office."

"I don't believe it!" Mrs. Smith said. She stood back and looked at him, all expression gone from her face. "I simply don't believe it. I think you must have lost your mind."

"It's true," he said, and there was pride in his voice. "They were thinking about sending Duffy, but they thought he wasn't reliable enough." He began talking hurriedly. "I'm to start a week from Saturday, and I'd like it if you and the girls would follow as soon as you can."

"New York," Mrs. Smith said slowly. "New York. Why, New York is a big city.

Not that St. Louis isn't big. It just doesn't seem big out here where we live. But New York! Why, what will the children do?"

"The same as they do here," he said. "Go to school, play, and have their friends over."

"What friends?" she asked.

"The friends they make at school," he answered.

"Rose is graduating this year," Mrs. Smith said. "Agnes is doing so well and sure to be promoted. Esther will be a senior. She's been dying to be a senior. And Tootie!"

"Tootie should have been in school this year," Mr. Smith said defiantly. "And would have been, too, if you hadn't carried on so about her being the baby. She'll have to start school sometime, you know."

"Naturally, I know," Mrs. Smith said. "But what did she learn that half-day we sent her to kindergarten? The children in that kindergarten couldn't even read. Tootie told me so. You know yourself that you thought it was pretty foolish to have her running around pretending to be a squirrel and singing that song about storing nuts away. Tootie's too smart for that."

"Tootie's too smart for her own good," Mr. Smith said. "She needs to have someone over her who'll put his foot down."

"Well, she ran right through the books Agnes had in the first grade in about a week. She said the print was too big and were the children all blind," Mrs. Smith said.

"There's no use talking," Mr. Smith said. "There it is. We're going to have to move."

Mrs. Smith moved still farther away from her husband. "And what are *you* getting out of it that you're so willing to move us lock, stock, and barrel to a perfectly strange place?" she asked.

"Now, listen, Anna," he said. "I've got the future to think about. Lon's in college. Next year, Esther will be ready for college. Rose has some damned notion about a finishing school. Tootie and Agnes will be in private schools. And I don't know how you've got it figured out, but I'd like to know where the money's coming from."

"Will you get a lot more pay?" Mrs. Smith asked.

"About a third more than I'm getting now," he said. "And if I build up a good business there, it might lead to anything." He got up from the chair quickly. "You'll have to break the news to the girls," he said.

"What about Katie?" Mrs. Smith asked. "What about Grandpa? What about the chickens? Not that we have many. As a matter of fact, I asked the iceman to kill one for us today. It was Bosco. She was getting so old and I thought she'd make a nice fricassee."

"Those are all things we can talk over later," Mr. Smith said. "I'm going to shave for dinner." He walked out of the room and up the front stairs without looking at her again.

Mrs. Smith stood still, her hands held tightly together and her lips quivering. Her face was white and she shut her eyes. Except for a faint rattle of pans in the kitchen, the house was still. She moved her feet and felt the carpet under them, the green Brussels carpet with the pink roses. With her eyes closed, she could see every detail of the living room, and she knew that she could lay her finger on every object in the house with her eyes blindfolded. The front door opened and she heard the voices of her four daughters.

ST. LOUIS *April 1904*

"Where's Mamma?" Agnes asked.

"I'm in here," Mrs. Smith said.

Tootie ran toward her, screaming, "I want to tell her first! I want to tell her first!"

"You told her first last time," Agnes said. "It's my turn to tell her first." She put her slender hand over Tootie's mouth, and Tootie bit it. Agnes leaned over and bit Tootie's arm.

"Stop that biting," Mrs. Smith said.

"Well, we saw the monitor Arkansas," Agnes said. "We all saw it. They told us at school that she was coming up the river, so I told Corinne, and Corinne told Tootie when she passed by on her way home. Otherwise, Tootie wouldn't have known anything about it and she would have missed it. That's why I think it's only fair that I should tell about it."

Mrs. Smith turned toward Tootie. "Do you mean to tell me that you went without asking?"

"I was playing down the street when Corinne told me," Tootie said. "I didn't have time. I ran over to the school and met Agnes, then she and I waited until the girls got out. *Then* we couldn't get Rose started. She was taking a picture of George. And we thought we'd never get there in time to see the monitor Arkansas coming in."

"I was taking a picture of George merely because the light was good and he happened to be the only male in sight," Rose said. "It was not on his account, I assure you. I hate, loathe, despise, abominate, and abhor him."

"Like fudge you do," Agnes said. "Anyway, it was grand. The whistles were blowing and the people were cheering and the girls were waving to the men and the men were waving back. Everybody was there."

"The monitor Arkansas is enormous," Tootie said.

"The most exciting part of the day was at school," Esther said. "While we were in the gym in the fifth hour swinging Indian clubs, who should Mr. Sears come in with but Governor Hogg of Texas and General Miles."

"General Miles is quite a big bug," Rose said. "He's Commander-in-Chief of the Army and he fought at Puerto Rico."

"Then," Esther said, "as though seeing such notable beings was not enough, when we came in from recess there they were, sitting on the platform, just as sweet and gracious as you please."

"The monitor Arkansas—" Tootie began.

"Shut up for a minute, Tootie," Esther said. "Well, Mamma, then Mr. Sears got up and made a speech of introduction. And then General Miles got up and made a talk and told us what an unusual *privilege* it was to address so many young ladies. And you bet he flattered us up fine—told us that he knew we all would grow up to be gracious, noble women, graceful, accomplished, educated, and gentle."

"And a thousand other things," Rose said. "Like that we would be the guiding stars in the communities where we lived. Honestly, I think these lady-fussers with gray hair are the *worst* kind."

"I don't think they were fussing at all," Esther said, patting her pompadour. "Anyhow, Governor Hogg got up—and he weighs about a ton—and made such a bright, witty speech, praising General Miles to the skies. He was truly humble in effacing himself. Then he said that General Miles was *our* servant and that all men in high official positions in this country were our servants. And then he asked Mr. Sears if he didn't think this was right. And, of course, Mr. Sears had to say yes. Then he asked Mr. Sears if he didn't think the majority should rule."

"And Mr. Sears had to say yes again," Rose said. "So then the Governor said, 'Well, I propose that we are dismissed this minute and that we are not to return until Monday morning. Do the majority agree with me?'"

"You can bet they did," Esther said. "Considering it's only Wednesday. And Mr. Sears couldn't boss the Governor after the Governor had impressed upon us that our early dismissal was in honor of his dear and distinguished friend General Miles."

"Well," Mrs. Smith said, "I'm glad you heard such inspiring speeches and saw the beautiful sight of the monitor Arkansas coming up the river." She sighed and sat down. "Because I have bad news for you. Your father's moving us all to New York."

Her daughters looked at her in stupefaction. Agnes was first to recover. "If you'll excuse me," she said, "I'll go and pack my dolls."

"I'll pack my dolls, too," Tootie said. "I'll

pack them all but Margaretha, and I'll carry her. She can ride in the little hammock on the train." She and Agnes started to leave the room.

"Come back here," Mrs. Smith said. "You're not packing any dolls *yet*. There are a great many things to talk over, and I must say, Agnes and Tootie, that you're very cool about it."

Rose and Esther continued to stare at their mother, then Esther broke into wild sobs. "Move to New York!" she cried. "I'll never move to New York. I've never seen the place and I never want to. What's Papa doing this to us for?"

"You mustn't blame your father too much," her mother said. "It means more money for him and, after all, you do want to go to college, Esther."

"Money!" Rose said coldly. "I hate, loathe, despise, abominate, and abhor money! Besides, how can I come out in New York where I don't know a soul? And those Eastern girls—it's a well-known fact that they're snobs."

"And the World's Fair," Esther said, her

eyes red. "Just when it's about to begin and just when St. Louis will be the center of attraction of the entire universe."

Agnes and Tootie stood staring at them. "You can see the Flatiron Building in New York," Agnes said. "And you can go to the Art Museum. I imagine the paintings that they have there day in and day out are finer than the ones they are going to show at the World's Fair. And I'd like to see the ocean."

"Don't be so silly," Rose said. "It won't look a bit different than Lake Michigan, and you see that every summer."

"It will look different to me," Agnes said.

"I want to hear all the people talk like Mr. Sears," Tootie said. She imitated him. "Awwah Fawthaw who awt in hev'n."

"You must not make fun of anyone who is saying the Lord's Prayer," Mrs. Smith said.

"She says her prayers like Mr. Sears every night," Agnes said. "Every single night since she got to go to the Christmas play."

"Well, she's to stop it," Mrs. Smith said.

"Agnes and Tootie are acting like imbeciles," Esther said. "I wish they'd keep out of this discussion. For instance, I think it's important to think of what will happen to Lady Babbie. And, I think Agnes should think of that, too. Lady Babbie is her cat."

"Lady Babbie!" Agnes cried. "Lady Babbie is coming with me in a basket lined with silk."

"And where are you going to keep her in New York?" Esther asked. "Cooped up in a tenement?"

"Don't they have houses in New York, for pity's sake?" Agnes asked.

"The rich people have houses," Rose said. "But the people like us have to live in sort of flats. There are hundreds of flats in one building. And they *rent* them."

Agnes drew closer to Rose and took her arm. "They *rent* them," she repeated. "You mean they have landlords like Mr. Johnson did before he bought his house?" Her eyes grew round and frightened. "I don't want to have anything to do with landlords," she said. "Tootie, we won't pack our things."

"No," Tootie said. "We won't. Anyway, I like it here. I guess I don't want to miss the World's Fair. I guess I don't want to live with a lot of other people."

"I simply won't go," Rose said. "Papa hasn't any right to ask me to."

"I won't go, either," Esther said. "Not that I don't want to help Papa if I can, but I could tell him a few things about the way Walter acted when he came back from New York. He's perfectly wicked at heart and hasn't been the same since. Mabel told me that his room is full of pictures of ballet girls, girls in tights, and his especial pride is a clown girl with one garter on."

"There's no use in discussing it, I suppose," Mrs. Smith said. "Your father's word seems to be law in this house. Now, get ready for dinner, if you have the heart to eat. The Lord knows I haven't."

After the girls went upstairs, Mrs. Smith got up and walked slowly through the dining room into the kitchen. In the kitchen she stood with her back to the door, the tears streaming down her face. The chicken was simmering slowly on the top of the new gas stove, which Katie kept shined and polished. She remembered the day it had come and how Lon had taken a time exposure of it. She looked around

ST. LOUIS *April 1904*

the kitchen, at the wainscoting around the walls, that had been painted ivory to blend with the soft brown of the woodwork, at the iron sink, with its filter attached to the cold-water faucet so that some of the mud that came from the river was caught in a fine sieve. The pantry door was open and she could see the small pasteboard barrel, gaily decorated with red roses, that contained gingersnaps. There was white, fresh paper edging on the shelves that had taken half a day to put on only the week before. Even the linoleum on the floor was new, and she remembered how often and how hard Katie had scrubbed the old wooden floor. In the rocking chair between the windows, Lady Babbie slept on an old cushion. Mrs. Smith went over and rubbed his head gently. At her touch he stretched his soft, strong legs and put out his claws. He opened his eyes until they were slits, and then closed them again. It was almost dark outside, but Mrs. Smith stood looking out of the window, seeing the boardwalk stretching down to the ashpit, the woodshed, and the chicken house. She remembered the hours Tootie had spent squeezing her thin little body in and out of the hole that had been cut in the door for the chickens. She could see the fruit trees, each one as individual as a person; there was the cherry tree that Esther had fallen from, the cherry tree with the straight, low branch that Agnes and Tootie played in; there were the two peach trees brought from Manitowoc and the new little Seckel pear.

Katie came into the kitchen, and Mrs. Smith turned her tear-stained face toward her. "Katie," she sobbed, "Katie," and felt comforting arms go around her.

"The girls told me," Katie said. "Holy Mary, what's to become of us all!"

Upstairs, Rose and Esther were in the bedroom they shared. Esther lay across the double bed and Rose walked nervously around the room. "I think I could give up anything easier than giving up our darling room," Rose said.

"I know," Esther said. "We've just finally got about everything we've wanted for it. It looks almost like a *stage* room."

"It does," Rose said softly. "It's about the prettiest room I ever saw. Of course, I don't doubt that Margaret's room might not be considered more elegant. But to me, it's too cold. She has no *things*. Just the things she needs on her bureau. You know, I don't call *that* a pretty room."

"And the way the sun comes in almost all day," Esther said. "And the way the honeysuckle vines have crept right *up* to the window."

"Yes. Remember we thought they never would?" Rose asked. "Of course, it isn't so bad for Tootie and Agnes. They don't remember when the house looked barer outside. Why, I remember when the maples were a lot smaller and the street wasn't nearly so shady."

"And when Grandpa brought the hammock home," Esther said.

"There's no denying it," Rose said. "No matter where we go, it won't be the same. Even if all the things are with us, it won't be the same." She flung herself down beside Esther and they held one another tight. Esther's tears felt warm against her sister's cheek.

Agnes and Tootie were in Grandpa Prophater's room. "New York's a nice enough place if you care for the kind of things they have there," he told them. "But you couldn't get me there on a bet."

"But you have to come, Grandpa," Agnes said. "You *have* to. What will you do?"

"Don't you worry about me," he said. "I might stay here in St. Louis somewhere, or I might go to New Orleans. There was a time I lived in New Orleans."

Tootie ran over to him and climbed on his lap. "No! No!" she cried. "Papa isn't the only one in this family. There are a whole lot of us. There are eight, not counting Papa. And we can write Lon. He'll never hear of us leaving. He'll send us a lot of money. Every time I really ask for money he gives me a quarter."

"Yes," Agnes said. "We are well-known people in this town. All the children come to this very house to play. We have the best fireworks on the Fourth of July, and we have the biggest tree in the whole city, I guess, on Christmas Day. People will think we're poor if we don't own anything and live in a flat."

"I wouldn't mind being poor if we could just stay here," Tootie said. "I would just as soon live with the orphalans, and play in that streetcar the streetcar people gave them. Rose says that children in New York wear hats. They're stuck up. I think it's stuck up to wear a hat except when you have to go to church."

The dinner bell rang downstairs. It rang only once and its tone seemed spiritless.

"Come along," Grandpa Prophater said to the two little girls. They walked past the door to Rose's and Esther's room. Rose opened the door and joined them. She was followed by Esther, whose eyes were now inflamed and swollen. As they walked down the stairs they formed a procession—a stubborn, resisting bloc.

Mr. Smith, hearing the dinner bell, got up from the bed, in which he had been lying. He heard the subdued sound of footsteps and the sound of a muffled sob. He straightened his tie and sighed. But he almost smiled when he thought of Duffy. He thought of having his own office, managing it, building up his business, and of the things that Anna and the girls could have—things they could never have if he stayed on in St. Louis.

He opened his door, walked briskly down the stairs, through the living room, and into the dining room. His wife was seated at the foot of the table, with Tootie beside her in the high chair. It was not as though Tootie needed to sit in a high chair, he knew. It was because she liked to swing the tray back and forth over her head. Just the same, she looked like a very little girl as she sat there. "Well!" he said. "I seem to be a little behind the parade."

Mrs. Smith rang the small silver bell that stood near her water glass, and Katie came into the room carrying a steaming platter filled with fricasseed chicken and dumplings.

"Well!" Mr. Smith said again. "This looks mighty fine!" He looked up at Katie and smiled. She turned her eyes away. He picked up a spoon and a fork. "The second joint for you, Anna?" he asked.

"Not tonight," Mrs. Smith said. "Just give me a little bit of the gravy. Just a spoonful."

Katie took the plate and set it before Mrs. Smith.

"Rose, the breast?" Mr. Smith asked.

"Not tonight, Papa," she said. "I'll have a little salad later, if there is any."

Mr. Smith set the fork and spoon down

heavily on the platter. "Now, see here—" he began.

"After dinner, Lonnie," Mrs. Smith said. She tore off a crust of bread and dipped it in the gravy.

When Mr. Smith had finished serving, the platter was still nearly full. Tootie had not fought with Agnes over the wings, and Agnes cut her wing with her knife and fork instead of picking it up in her fingers as she usually did. Tootie broke the silence. "You know what I think I'll do tomorrow?" she said. "I think I'll dig a tunnel from the side of the terrace right straight *in* and see where I come out. I wouldn't be surprised if I came out across the streetcar tracks on the side of the Middletons' terrace, because they're directly in back of us. And when I have it finished and Mrs. Middleton is walking around some day the way she does on that lawn of hers, I'll grab her by the leg."

"It will take months," Agnes said.

"I don't care," Tootie said. "I don't care how long it takes so long as I come out in the right place and can surprise Mrs. Middleton by grabbing ahold of her leg."

"You won't have time," Agnes said.

"I've got plenty of time," Tootie said.

"Not if you get moved away," Agnes said,

Tootie looked down the table at her father, "I won't move until I get it finished," she said firmly, looking him straight in the eyes.

"Don't use that impudent tone with your father," Mrs. Smith said sharply.

"She's not using an impudent tone," Agnes said. "She's stating a fact. She just means she isn't going to be dragged out of her own home and sent away like a—well, like a Huguenot!"

Esther began to cry softly and Rose held her napkin to her lips. She leaned over and patted her father's hand. "It *is* hard, Papa," she said. "But we'll all get used to it. We don't want you to worry."

Mr. Smith grabbed the fork and spoon from the platter and plunged them into the fricassee. "No one's going to make any sacrifices for me!" he said. "I'm not going to have to creep in and out of my own home for the next day, week, or year like a damned thief! The hell with Duffy, and the hell with everybody! Now, pass your plates and eat the food you're lucky to get!"

There was a stunned silence.

"Aren't we going, Papa?" Agnes asked after a while.

"No, by God," he said. "We're staying right here until we rot."

Mrs. Smith passed her plate up the table to have it filled. "We won't rot," she said. "We haven't yet."

Katie, listening in the kitchen, heard the clatter of the dishes and the sound of voices and laughter. She picked Lady Babbie from the chair near the window and sat down with the cat in her lap. "Bless the Lord and all the saints," she said quietly, as though the kitchen were a church.

May 1904

MAY 1904

The miracle of the World's Fair in St. Louis, rising as it did out of the wilderness, stunned everyone. It seemed impossible that only two years before, Governor Francis of Missouri had driven in the first stake with a silver ax while crowds walking through the briers and coarse grass to witness the ceremony carried heavy sticks to protect themselves from snakes. The enthusiasm of the press was unlimited, and verses appeared daily in the newspapers.

The greatest show that ever showed
Will rise beside the Skinker Road.

The buildings were elegant and formal and were constructed in the approved palatial style. There was no thought of dynamic expression or crude force in back of anything. The force was refined. There were no statues of workmen adorning the buildings, no bits of machinery were glorified in the exhibits. Greek goddesses presided over the domes, classic and beautiful. The savages, the Igorots, the Moros, the Bagobos, and Fiji Islanders, had been brought there to be stared at and not to be educated. And bandstands were everywhere. Bands from Bolivia, Honduras, Colombia, dressed in green, yellow, and scarlet. The Philippine constabulary ranged over the place. There seemed to be millions of them—small brown men in uniform, constantly hurrying. And the grounds were filled with girls—girls in the daytime in linen skirts and bolero jackets, pink, blue, yellow, and lavender, in white embroidered hats and bows to match their suits; girls in the evening in flowered organdies, who danced in the various state buildings with West Point cadets or laughed, looked on, and ate chicken salads at Mrs. Rohrer's. To the people of St. Louis, the Fair was finished, perfect. It was the cream of everything in the world. There was nothing better to come. Only the visitors complained of the mud, and the West Point Year Book ran a verse.

Ach, St. Louis,
Ach, St. Louis,
Your name's mud,
Thick and gooey.

ST. LOUIS *May 1904*

After the opening the cultural excitement died down somewhat and people began to enjoy the Fair. They paid high prices for things and boasted about it, and what they got free they enjoyed and were silent.

A few weeks after the Fair had opened the Smith family sat at the breakfast table. It was Saturday, and they talked excitedly. "Tootie and Agnes can go with Grandpa," Mrs. Smith said. "The girls and Lon can go along with their friends. And Papa and I will get off when we can. I think it's too much to go all together."

"I don't want to go with Tootie," Agnes said. "She hasn't any interest in it, really. She wants to stay on the Pike all the time, or ride on the camels."

"I would just as soon stay home and play," Tootie said mildly. "Helen Ferris and I made a discovery yesterday. We discovered that if we start at the top of Union Hill just when we hear the brewery horses driving through the alley halfway down, we can skate right under their noses when they come out into the street."

Agnes put down her spoon. "You're a horrible girl, Tootie Smith," she said. "You might run right into those horses and hurt them."

Tootie drank her cocoa from a saucer. "We never hit them. We didn't hit them at all," she said.

"You'll go with your grandfather," Mrs. Smith said to Tootie. "I'm not going to have you carried home on a stretcher when there's no one here to take care of you."

"Then I'll go with Corinne," Agnes said. "We've decided that we'll call it the Louisiana Purchase Exposition, which it really is, instead of the World's Fair. We think World's Fair doesn't sound as nice."

"Well, Rose and I are going to see the Princeton track team with Lon," Esther said. "Just think of the bad luck! If Lon weren't a freshman, he'd probably have been running in front of all those people."

"Maybe," Lon said. "By the way, Agnes, Bob Harris was asking for you yesterday."

"Bob Harris!" Agnes gasped. "He never was!"

Rose raised her eyes. "Who on earth is Bob Harris?" she asked.

"He's a member of the Kwakiutl tribe,"

Agnes answered loftily. "His real name is Klakoglas, and it means 'Man who has copper.' I met him for the first time day before yesterday. He's not as good-looking as Charles James Nowell. He's a member of the tribe, too. But Bob Harris is the friendliest."

"Didn't anybody ask for me?" Tootie said.

Lon frowned and nodded. "I heard Bulon, the Chief of the Bagobos, mentioning your name," he said. "He was sharpening an ugly-looking knife and the rest of the Bagobos were dancing around, swinging their bolos and beating tom-toms. I wouldn't go near him today if I were you. He's getting ugly."

"I didn't do a thing to him," Tootie said. "And he has beautiful hair three feet long."

Mrs. Smith got up from the table. "Well," she said. "Suppose we all meet by the steps at Festival Hall at nine this evening. Then we can see the lights, and then Papa and I, the children and Grandpa can come home. Lon, you see that the girls are all right."

"They'll be all right," Lon said.

"Corinne and I are going to look at the paintings," Agnes said, "and then we're going to spend the rest of our time in the Liberal

Arts Building." She got up and left the table, the skirt of her black-and-white plaid jumper dress swishing from side to side.

Rose walked to the window and stood looking out across the side yard. The weeping birch was in full leaf and the snowball bush was in bloom. "A day like today is divine," she said. "I feel absolutely scintillating."

"Well, scintillate yourself upstairs and get ready," Lon said.

Esther stood up and put her arm lightly around Lon's shoulder. "Lon," she said sweetly, "do you mind if Ida Boothby comes along with us? You know how Rose is! She'll be snapped up right off the bat by a crowd of West Pointers, especially Douglas Moore. And they consider us too *young*. So if you'll just stay with us until maybe we meet someone we know, that's all we'll ask."

"Who is Ida Boothby?" Lon asked.

"She's a girl Esther met," Rose said. "She's from Joplin, Missouri. She's a nice little thing. Her folks are down for the fair."

"She's not pretty, exactly," Esther said. "But she's real cute. She's staying with the Dodges, and we can stop by on our way to the trolley and pick her up."

ST. LOUIS *May 1904*

"All right," Lon said. "Hurry up."

He stepped out onto the back porch. The air was soft and the sun was already beating down. There wasn't a cloud in the sky. Lon took his pipe out of his pocket, filled and lit it. The smoke curled around him in the still air and finally disappeared. He thought of the summer that lay ahead, of the long, hot evenings and the thunderstorms that sometimes flashed and cracked for an hour before the hot rain fell, and subsided, leaving the city steaming and torrid. He supposed Rose would be taken up with her new West Point beau and there wouldn't be so many evenings spent around the piano as there had been. Since he had got home he hadn't touched his mandolin once. He turned and went back into the house and into the front hall, where his mandolin case stood in the corner by the piano. He opened the case, took the mandolin out, and picked at the strings. The instrument was out of tune, and he held it near his ear, turning the keys and touching each string with his tortoise-shell pick. Then he put the mandolin back in the case.

It was cool and quiet in the hall. The front door stood open and a yellow butterfly fluttered outside the screen. The leaves of the honeysuckle vine had opened and there were a few flowers on the vine. The sun, striking the wooden steps, was almost blinding. Katie had turned the hose on the porch earlier in the day, but now it was almost dry, and small pools of water stood only where the steps had sagged in the middle. The iceman's wagon had stopped next door and the horse stamped his hoofs on the brick street and twitched his tail, impatient with the flies. Down the block, Lon could hear the sound of roller skates and the strawberry man's voice as he called, "Strawberries, nice strawberries." He listened to the chant of five notes and hummed them to himself. Although it was only May, he thought the street smelled of summer, of fruit, watermelon, and cool cucumbers. It was a smell that made him homesick, even as he stood there. He wondered what they would do at the Fair that day before and after the track meet. All the girls in town would be at the track meet, and their eyes would be worshipping. They worshipped anything, he thought. Rose and her friends considered it a disgrace to be without a West Point escort, although they pretended to be excited over the fact that so many of the boys they had known all winter were working in the concessions at the Fair. He turned away from the door and called up the stairs, "Get a move on!"

Esther and Rose came down the stairs. They were pretty and their clothes were clean and starched. Rose wore a deep-pink linen skirt, a white blouse under her jacket, and a white hat trimmed with a pink bow. Esther wore a white skirt, with a red bow in her hat and a red belt. They smelled of violets.

Lon took his hat from the hatrack and followed his sisters down the porch steps. Walking along the sidewalk with the girls fluttering at his side, he felt dull and apathetic. As they neared the Dodges' house they heard the sound of a piano.

"That's Ida," Esther said. "She plays some. She sings too. She sings very well."

"She doesn't sing anywhere nearly as well as you do, Ess," Rose said. "Her voice isn't as high. She sings a good alto, though."

They stopped in front of the house to listen. The Dodges' porch looked different, somehow, Lon thought. Someone had run a blue ribbon through the back of one of the wicker rockers, and by the side of the rocker there was a guitar tied with a large blue bow.

"Ida!" Esther called. "Sing it!"

"All right!" Ida called back. She began to sing "Nut-Brown Maiden." Her voice was low and true.

As she started to sing the second verse, Lon stepped up to the porch and sang through the screen door a parody of the song:

Nut-brown maiden, I love thy pearly, pearly teeth.
Nut-brown maiden, I love thy pearly teeth.
Thy pearly teeth are false, love,
They rattle when you waltz, love.
Nut-brown maiden, I love thy pearly teeth.

Ida swung around on the piano stool and stared at him through the screen, humming the tune with him. She saw a thin young man with light-brown hair. When the song was finished she came to the screen and opened it. As she stood there with the sun shining on her, Lon thought he had never seen a prettier girl. She was small and brown-skinned and her hair was brown, without a trace of red in it.

"This is my brother, Lon," Esther said. "Lon, I want you to meet my friend, Miss Boothby."

Ida Boothby smiled and nodded her head. "I've never heard *that* version," she said to Lon. "I don't think those are very nice words for such a pretty song." She moved away from the door, and in a few minutes she was back, holding her hat in her hand. She wore a brown linen skirt with no coat, and the hat she carried was made of brown leghorn with brown velvet ribbons. "I'll put it on when I get there," she said. "In Joplin we don't go in for hats much."

They started down the street to the trolley. Lon walked in front with Rose, and Esther and Ida trailed along behind. "She's a sweet little thing," Rose said.

"She's just a kid," Lon said. "She looks younger than Ess."

"That's just her way," Rose said. "She's no *younger*. As a matter of fact, I think she's older."

On the trolley, Rose sat down near the window and motioned to Esther to sit beside her. As the car started, Ida lurched to the side and Lon caught her by the arm. They laughed and moved to a seat nearer the front. The window was open, and Ida leaned out and let the wind blow through her hair. Her hair was short and curly and was caught into a knot at the top of her head. She wore no pompadour. "I'm disgracefully tanned," she said.

"What of it?" Lon said. "The girls here are scared of a little tan. You look all right tanned. You look like a pecan."

"Esther tells me you are a Princeton man," she said.

Lon blushed. "What's your favorite college?" he asked.

She glanced at him through her lashes. "Princeton," she said.

At the fairgrounds, they made their way through the crowds to the Plaza of St. Louis, where Rose had promised to meet Douglas Moore. Ida walked beside Lon. It was cool at the Plaza and the mist from the fountains blew into her face. She stood back from the Lagoon and looked up at the statue of St. Louis mounted upon a Norman horse. The statue guarded the gates to the great central plaza of the exposition, and St. Louis held high the cross hilt of his sword. Nearby were equestrian statues of Joliet and De Soto. The four young people breathed in the cool air.

"Here he is," Rose said. "Here's Mr. Moore. He's got somebody with him."

Esther looked at her sister, suspicion in her eyes. "If you—" she began.

"I didn't say a word, I assure you," Rose said.

The two young men were out of breath. "Good morning, Miss Smith," Douglas Moore said to Rose. "I hope we haven't kept you waiting. We've been parading and it held us up. Miss Smith, I'd like you to meet my brother John. He's not a West Pointer now, but he will be in the fall."

John Moore was smaller than his brother and very blond. He glanced admiringly at Rose, but it was plain that his real interest lay in the two younger girls. He looked Ida Boothby over and, seeing that she was standing close to Lon, he discarded her and turned to Esther, pleased and excited. "I hoped you were going to turn out to be the one," he said.

The girls screamed, and Ida Boothby called out "Well, I like that, I must say!"

Rose gave a last little laugh and fanned

her face with her handkerchief. "Now, suppose we decide what to do," she said.

"Well, if Miss Esther doesn't mind, it's Asia for me," John Moore said.

"Oh, I adore Asia," Esther said. "And I've never ridden on the camels."

"*I* would like to stroll around," Rose said. "And then maybe have some Scotch scones."

"I think it would be nice to see *all* the state buildings," Ida Boothby said. "I haven't been in one of them."

"All right," Douglas Moore said. "We'll make it this way. I'll stroll with Miss Smith. And John and Esther and Lon and Miss Boothby can do what they want to do. And if we don't meet at the track meet, where can we meet?"

"Well, we promised our family that we would meet them at nine by Festival Hall," Rose said. "Of course, nine is awfully long, and we may get tired of one another."

They laughed hilariously at this and started out across the Plaza.

Tootie skipped by Grandpa Prophater's side. "Let's see the Galveston Flood again, shall we?" she asked. "Let's see it as many times as we can and then go on to the Pike." She shifted a handful of spun sugar from one hand to the other and looked up at him. "We're really right by the Galveston Flood," she said.

Grandpa Prophater looked toward the building, which had "GALVESTON FLOOD" in large letters across the front, and sighed. Then he put his hand in his pocket, rattling his loose change, and walked through the archway, holding Tootie by one sticky hand. They sat down and waited for the theatre to grow dark. Tootie sat forward on her seat, her eyes staring fixedly at the curtain. "How much did it cost to make this?" she asked.

"A lot of money," Grandpa Prophater said. "About fifty or sixty thousand dollars."

"Golly!" Tootie said.

The house grew dark and the curtain rose. At the foreground there were grass, trees, and fences of real material, and in back of these was a canvas painted to represent the city of Galveston and the Galveston beach. The beach had real water washing up on it, and farther out to sea the waves rolled. Boats moved in and out of the harbor. Little streetcars ran along the streets and trains ran across the trestlework spanning Galveston Bay. The day closed with wonderful cloud effects and the sun set a blazing track across the ocean. As the sunlight faded, Tootie gripped her grandfather's arm. "Here it comes now!" she whispered. "Here it comes! Here's where the storm begins." The dark clouds gathered and the gale began. The water rose and the waves increased in size until the water filled the streets. The fury of the storm grew until a mist enveloped the whole city and a dreadful roaring sound filled the air. Suddenly the rain stopped and the waves rolled back. Ships lay strewn on the beach and the city was shown in ruins. The stage grew dark again, and then the new Galveston was revealed, salvaged and rebuilt from the disaster.

Tootie stood up. "I don't like it when the city gets all fixed again," she said. "I like it when it's flooded and horrible."

"You wouldn't like it if you were there," Grandpa Prophater said. He snorted and looked down at her as she wriggled through the crowds like an eel. "At that," he added, "you might like it. You'd probably live through it, too."

"Now the Pike?" she asked.

He took a worn five-dollar bill from his pocket. "Now the Pike," he said. He spoke with an air of happy anticipation.

Agnes and Corinne stood in front of a painting of Mary Magdalene. "I'm tired," Corinne said. "And I think we should have something to eat."

"Don't bother me when I'm taking notes," Agnes said. "That's the Cross of Jesus." She looked at the lovely arms of Mary Magdalene as she knelt at the foot of the Cross, and at her hands, that caressed the feet of her Saviour.

Corinne stood dumbly in front of the picture, and as Agnes turned away she repeated, "I do think we ought to eat."

"We'll eat as soon as we look at 'Beneath the Beech.' We have to stand in front of it for twenty minutes at least," Agnes said.

"We've stood in front of them all for twenty minutes," Corinne said.

"Do you want to come out of here with nothing?" Agnes asked. "Unless you stand twenty minutes in front of a work of art, you come out with nothing."

They moved toward the Belgian section of the Palace of Arts, and Agnes looked around until she found the painting she had been looking for. It showed a flock of sheep feeding in the shade of a huge beech tree. A shepherdess watched over the flock.

"Those don't look like leaves to me," Corinne said. "They look like blots of paint."

"You have to pretend they're leaves," Agnes said. "I can pretend easy. I never saw anyone who could pretend less than you. Even Tootie can see anything she wants to."

They stood in front of the painting for exactly twenty minutes by Agnes's small watch, and then moved on.

It was after nine when Mr. and Mrs. Smith got to Festival Hall. They had decided to stay home after all and had taken the trolley to the fairgrounds in the cool of the evening. It was still twilight and the lights were not turned on. "I hope they get here before the electricity begins," Mrs. Smith said. "It is almost ghostly to see it."

ST. LOUIS *May 1904*

To their right they saw Grandpa Prophater and Tootie. Grandpa was walking slowly, but Tootie danced and skipped at his side. He walked up to his daughter and turned his pockets inside out. "Well, Annie," he said. "She cleaned me."

"Have you had any dinner?" Mrs. Smith asked.

"No," he said. "But we've had everything else. So don't ask me if I'm hungry. I never expect to be hungry again."

"We went in this place, Mamma," Tootie said. "This place on the Pike. There was a girl in there with a spangled dress that came to her knees. She had on a lot of ruffles, too. And she had her face all painted up to look pretty. We stayed and saw her three times."

"Father!" Mrs. Smith said.

Grandpa Prophater shrugged his shoulders. "I didn't want to stay," he said. "She was the one. She knows the whole act and all the words to the song."

"I do. That's right," Tootie said. "It's called 'Teasing.' It goes, 'Teasing, teasing, I was only teasing you.' I'm going to do it all for Lon. He'll like it."

May 1904

Agnes came running along the cement path toward her mother. "Mamma!" she cried breathless. "Guess what they have. It's the best you ever saw. I mean it's the best of them all. It's a black-and-white chicken and a red barn, and it might just as well be at Grandma's. I liked it much better than the odalisques. And I wrote down a beautiful description of it. It's by a man named Zorn. Just a black-and-white chicken. I suppose it was his favorite and he painted its portrait."

Mrs. Smith drew her arm around Agnes and pulled her close to her skirts. "You're tired," she said. "And where is Corinne?"

"Her!" Agnes exclaimed. "*She* got tired. She doesn't care anything about paintings. All she thinks is eat, eat, eat."

"Didn't you get a bite *anywhere*?" Mrs. Smith asked.

"I ate some ice cream," Agnes said. "I spent the rest of my money on postcards they sell at the Palace of Arts."

In couples, the rest of the family arrived, Lon with Ida, Rose with Douglas Moore, and Esther hanging onto John Moore's arm and laughing foolishly. They stood talking and laughing, waiting for the lights to go on.

ST. LOUIS *May 1904*

Lon hummed "Nut-Brown Maiden" into Ida's ear, and she smiled. "But with the *right* words," she said.

"The right words," he repeated. He never remembered feeling half so happy before in his life. And he wondered that a girl as feminine as Ida would go to the Transportation Palace with him, a building that suggested a magnificent railroad terminal.

"Mamma," Rose said, "Mr. Moore has asked me to West Point next winter. Don't you think I might say yes?"

Mrs. Smith gave a sharp glance toward Mr. Moore. He was a nice-looking boy, she thought. "Ask your father, Rose," she said.

"I think it would be more than all right," John Moore said. "Especially if Miss Esther were allowed to come, too."

"Well—" Mrs. Smith began as tiny sparks of light outlined the Cascades, Festival Hall, and the Colonnade of States. Suddenly the outlines of the columns, the arches, and the great statues were obliterated entirely. The lights glowed in dull redness and expanded into white light. It was as though the picture had been rebuilt in a minute, not of substance but of light. The successive falls of the Cascades shone in the brilliance. The white lights faded out and from bottom to top, from end to end, the Festival Hall, the Colonnade, and the Pavilions stood out in carmine.

Everyone stopped talking, and Rose drew in her breath sharply. "There never has been anything like it in this world," she said. "There never will be."

Mr. Smith put his arm around his wife's waist and Tootie and Agnes clung to Grandpa Prophater. "And just think," Mrs. Smith said, her voice soft and awe-stricken. "It's all right here where we live."

"Right by the old Skinker Road," Mr. Smith said.

"I remember when the road didn't amount to a hill of beans," Grandpa Prophater said.

"It's where we live," Agnes repeated. "We don't have to visit here. We don't have to come on a train, or stay at a hotel, or anything. They won't ever tear it down, will they?"

"No," Tootie said. "They will never tear it down. It will be like this forever."

"I can't believe it," Agnes said. "Right here where we live. Right here in St. Louis."